Falling Forward

A GIRL'S JOURNEY FROM THE UGLY CRY TO THE CROWN OF LIFE

Andrea Hernandez

TRILOGY CHRISTIAN PUBLISHERS

TUSTIN, CA

Trilogy Christian Publishers
A Wholly Owned Subsidiary of Trinity Broadcasting Network
2442 Michelle Drive
Tustin, CA 92780

Falling Forward: A Girl's Journey from the Ugly Cry to the Crown of Life

Trilogy Christian Publishers A Wholly Owned Subsidiary of Trinity Broadcasting Network

2442 Michelle Drive Tustin, CA 92780

Cover design by Jeff Summers

For information about special discounts for bulk purchases, please contact Trilogy Christian Publishing.

Trilogy Disclaimer: The views and content expressed in this book are those of the author and may not necessarily reflect the views and doctrine of Trilogy Christian Publishing or the Trinity Broadcasting Network.

Manufactured in the United States of America

10 9 8 7 6 5 4 3 2 1

Library of Congress Cataloging-in-Publication Data is available.

ISBN: 978-1-68556-348-6

E-ISBN: 978-1-68556-349-3

Dedication

This book is dedicated to you; you're the reason I wrote this. I am cheering for you, praying for you. I declare that you will have victory over whatever the enemy brings against you because you are victorious in Christ, you are righteous in Christ, and you are so very loved.

Acknowledgements

Thank You, God, for protecting me from what I thought I wanted and for blessing me with what I didn't know I needed. Thank You that You never stopped pursuing this prodigal daughter of Yours and for showing me what real love is. Thank You for Your Son, Jesus Christ, my Lord and Savior, and for Your sacrifice on the cross. Thank You for Your precious Holy Spirit.

Thank you to New Life Family Church. To my pastors, thank you for leading us and showing us a true example of love and humility. To all my spiritual family, I love you. My forever homegroup (Gabe, Zandra, Jackie, Zule, Leo, Madai, Erica) for being an amazing support system. Jackie and Priscilla, I wouldn't be here without you guys; I love you with my whole heart, you guys were so pivotal to my walk with God, and for you, I am eternally thankful. Karen Dorado, aka grammar queen. Audrey Muñoz, for paving the way for me; you're a fierce woman of God, and your life is a precious gift to many.

Jacklyn and Luis Ochoa, for your obedience in starting Roots Young Adults Ministry. Thank you for being God-fearing leaders and always being there to point me back to the truth, even when it hurts. Finally, thank you to my parents for loving me. Even though we were never wordy people, I want to tell you that I love you so much. I wouldn't be who I am today without your love and support throughout my life, for your constant provision for my brother and I when we didn't have anything. I am and will always be your little girl. ¡Los amo!

Contents

Introduction

Before I begin, I want to clarify that I felt in no way qualified to write a book. Believe me when I tell you that I prayed fervently for God to give me a beautiful singing voice so that I could honor Him through song and worship instead. This is my worship.

My prayer for you is that through reading this book about my life experiences and God's unfailing love and faithfulness in them, you might relate and be encouraged to draw near to God. This book is not about tackling the world's problems. This book is about getting to know the truth about ourselves and bringing our problems and hurts to light to begin the healing process in our lives and lead us to an intimate relationship with God. I know this can be extremely difficult to do. I may not know you, but I pray for you and can only imagine the pain and hurts that you have been through, my friend. Each of us has our own battles—some of which no one else knows about. Life is hard, even crushing at times.

Even in our deepest pains, rejections, and disappointments, God promises that He will be there with us. Hebrews 13:5 (NIV) says: "Never will I leave you. Never will I forsake you."

God heals broken hearts and bandages up *all* our wounds. At times, we don't see how God is orchestrating in our lives. Through every trial, God's hand has always held on to me and refused to let me go, even when I rejected Him. I believe with my whole heart that God loves us and has an amazing purpose for you, me, and every one of us. His will is better than anything that we could ever imagine.

I am the furthest away from being perfect, but because of God's love and redemption, I am here, able to share with you. I will be raw and real with you. Follow me on this journey from heartbreak, rejection, and more heartbreak to falling at the feet of my loving Father. These testimonials are not in chronological order, and names have been changed for identity purposes.

Like with me, God can take anyone's feelings of brokenness and turn their life into something beautiful. Is the process pain-free? No, but it is worth it.

Here are a few details for you to be aware of as you read this book: my intention is for you to read this as if we were sitting at our local coffee shop (ahem, He Brews Life Café) having a sugar-free vanilla latte with oat milk sipping and sharing our hearts with each other. Maybe one day we will, and I will get to hear your testimony. Some references to the Bible have been paraphrased for context, but please take everything that I say and test it with the truth that is the Word of God, aka the Bible. I share my heart in this book, and I in no way try to glorify sin; I have come a long way, and I am sharing what God has brought me out of. I want you to know that I have been praying for you, even before you received this book. I pray that it blesses you and that God speaks to you as you relate to my stories. We are in this together; I love you (hope that's not weird. If it is, then, oh well, I will tell you again, I love you!).

CHAPTER 1

Wave Watchers

On a particular Sunday after church a few years ago, two of my girlfriends and I made the short commute to the beach nearby. The day was perfect. The sun was out, the skies were clear, and the ocean water was therapeutically warm. We watched the waves toss back and forth. We soaked up the radiant sun, which due to Texas heat, turned us into extremely sunburned ladies within minutes—not an exaggeration. If you know, you know.

We stationed our canopy in a very hip beach location. I would be lying if I said that we weren't people-watching too. To my left, a group of people seemed to be having the time of their lives. The group was under a canopy with Latin music blasting that was so contagious that made everyone want to dance, even me with my two left feet. It was obvious that all the individuals had consumed more than a couple. Up to a few years ago, I was no stranger to alcohol or its effects until I arrived at the realization that alcohol only brought darkness to my life. I know there are people who are responsible when it comes to alcohol; I was never one of those.

The party next to us continued to grow in size and in ambiance. An attractive man could be seen flirting with a couple of girls from the group. In that moment, I began to reflect on all the times I had been in nearly identical situations. A few years ago, I would have been one of those giddy girls striving for the attention of an "alpha male."

I looked over to the waves and exhaled: "Thank You, Jesus." Let me explain: I felt gratitude that I was in a place where I was totally full and satisfied in my current season of life. I had joy, and despite recent heartbreaks, I was full and not lacking anything.

In my younger years, I was a slave to culture. I wanted all the things that I was told would make me happy. I tried everything from diet pills, excessive workouts, provocative clothing, fancy career, and material items to gain approval of the world, but I still felt empty. I now know that my identity does not come from any status or possessions but from God. I still struggle sometimes, but every day I make the conscious decision to die to my desires, pick up my cross, and follow Jesus because therein lies true freedom. I have come to realize that I live in this place called Earth, but I know that this is not my home. This is temporary, and my home is in eternity in heaven with God.

I do not know where you are today in life, but I want to share with you that there is purpose in you picking up this book. Perhaps you can relate to me trying everything to fill a void. Perhaps you feel lonely, unworthy, anxious, depressed, and not enough. I want to tell you that you are not alone. We all have that feeling or void that you feel. In fact, it was placed by God Himself. I know it sounds weird; let me explain with this scripture from Ecclesiastes 3:11 (NIV): "He has made everything beautiful in its time. Also he has put eternity into a man's heart, yet so that he cannot find out what God has done from the beginning to the end."

Confused still? I was too. I have come to understand that when the Bible says that God put eternity in a man's heart, it means that we will never be completely satisfied with earthly pleasures and pursuits. We have eternal value. Nothing but the eternal God can truly satisfy us.

I feel that in our culture, we are always looking forward to the next stage of our lives, making ourselves believe that when we have certain things, whether material or relational, we will begin our lives and then be happy. The consumer mentality robs us of so much joy and happiness. It is a human race. When I had this epiphany, I didn't want to race anymore; I just wanted to be.

I used to be like the waves I watched at the beach that Sunday afternoon with my girlfriends, tossed one way and then another. I used to follow wherever the world told me to go and not live a life in peace and knowledge of the real truth. As a person who constantly tries to be in control, letting go was and is at times an acquired behavior that comes with plenty of resistance. Once you do let go, let me tell you that there is such a freakishly supernatural peace that comes from casting all your worries on the Lord.

Although you may be facing difficult life moments at the moment, remember Romans 8:28 (NIV): "We know that in all things God works for the good of those who love him, who have been called according to his purpose."

I do not know what purpose God has for you, but I know that you are oh so loved. If you are reading this, it means that you are alive and breathing with a pulse, and you have a purpose. We all do. In our trials, we grow the most. God calls us out into the uncomfortable, but we can cast our worries on the Lord.

Allow God into your heart and let Him fill that void. Keep moving forward, toward Jesus, fixing your eyes on Him and His Word.

Crowning Moment

I do not have to be like the waves of the world tossed one side or another. I have certainty in the Word of God to lead me to the truth and my real identity.

Armor of Choice: Belt of Truth (The Word of God)

When you know the Truth, the Truth sets you free. We have the Word of God to be able to stand on God's truth and not be deceived by the lies and standards of the world.

Verse to Remember

"If any of you lacks wisdom, let him ask God, who gives generously to all without reproach, and it will be given to him. But let him ask in faith, with no doubting, for the one who doubts is like a wave of the sea that is driven and tossed by the wind" (James 1:5–6, NIV).

CHAPTER 2

Holy Spirit Fire

I was driving, and a memory came back to me. My pastor once mentioned how the word "remember" is written in the Bible over three hundred times. It made sense to me because we, as humans, tend to be forgetful. We complain and groan about our lives, and that is exactly what the Israelites did. God had taken them out of slavery in Egypt. He parted the Red Sea so they could flee from Pharaoh, and soon after, they were complaining and begging to go back. I am guilty of judging the Israelites. It is usually when I find myself being judgmental that God is quick to remind me of times that He has revealed Himself to me, and I still chose to be disobedient.

Not too long ago, as a "maturing" Christian, I had a conversation with a friend where I became resentful toward her. She had grown up in the gospel and had been raised the "right" way. I would think, *Well, if she knew the truth, why didn't she share Jesus?* I kept thinking and wanting to place blame on her and other young Christians that were around me for not sharing Jesus sooner. *Maybe*, I thought, *if they had shared about Jesus and His love for me, then I wouldn't have made millions of bad decisions that ultimately led me to pain and further away from Christ.* I was being dramatic and feeling sorry for myself when one of my friends stopped me and said, "Andy, it doesn't matter how you got here; it matters that you did. Even before creation, God chose you. He made you fearfully and wonderfully. God created you with a purpose, and from the very beginning, the enemy has been out to get you. That is what he does: he tries to get you at a young age to hurt you, discourage you before you realize your worth and identity. The devil wanted to get you as far away from the will of God so that you won't be effective for God's kingdom. He has been coming at you hard because his time here on earth is coming to an end. I know you wish you would have gotten it sooner; we all do. The beautiful part in all of this is that now you can become the woman you needed to other girls and women."

In those moments that I was feeling sorry for myself, I felt a nudge in my heart. God took me back to when I was nineteen. My mom became part of a women's non-denominational prayer group. This group's focus was a relationship with Christ as the foundation of everything, regardless of religion. I began attending their reunions even though it was an older crowd. I was inspired listening to the women in these groups share their testimonies of God's faithfulness in their lives, and I craved it too. I did start seeing the changes in my life when I started what I believed was my "walk" with God. I had an understanding that I had accepted Christ into my heart as my Lord and Savior, but I left it at that. I didn't fully know or understand what it was like to walk with Christ. I always stayed at Calvary. I knew that I was a sinner; I would repent, confess, then sin again. This was the cycle I was in for the longest time.

Through that organization, I was invited to a youth retreat in Guanajuato, Mexico. The retreat was in one of the most beautiful places in Mexico, surrounded by mountains and greenery. The weather was perfect, and we were staying in a hacienda that looked more like an enchanted castle. Everyone there seemed to be on fire for Jesus, except me. I was the skeptical one out of the whole place. My heart was hardened. I saw these young adults like myself and judged them for being fanatical about Jesus. I would think, *Okay, I love Jesus, but I am not crazy like them.* Look at me now. If I really loved Jesus then, I would have been obedient to Him. The weekend was filled with testimonies and team-bonding exercises that constantly talked about God's goodness and faithfulness, and I still missed it. It stormed one of the nights, so instead of us sleeping in the tents, we were moved inside. The next night, we took a hike about a mile out from the "castle." We arrived at an open field surrounded by mountains. The moon was so bright, which left us without a need for flashlights. The stars were the brightest that I had ever seen; they felt as if they were literally on top of me. The fields smelled like that of fresh rain on the grass. In the center of the field, there was a huge bonfire pit. It was filled with firewood. The host family and some of the workers said that even though it was our "bonfire night," there was a very real possibility that the wood wouldn't light because of how wet it was. They attempted to light the bonfire. It was a while before they were able to get a spark. We were sitting in a giant circle anxiously waiting. We *all* wanted that fire to burn; our feet were wet from the muddy hike, and the temperature was in the low 60s Fahrenheit. We waited in silence. Then, somewhere in the circle at a distance, someone started to sing. The song was in Spanish; it is called "Enciende una luz" by Marcos Witt.

Enciende una luz, déjala brillar,
la luz de Jesús que brille en todo lugar.
No la puedes esconder, no te puedes callar,
ante tal necesidad, enciende una luz en la oscuridad.[1]

---

1 Marcos Witt, "Enciende una luz," track 11 on Enciende Una Luz, Canzion Group LP, 1999.

Turn on a light, let it shine,
Let the light of Jesus shine everywhere.
You can't hide it, you can't be silent,
In the face of such a need, light a light in the dark

The spark that was lit became a flame; we continued to sing. The entire firewood became engulfed in flames before we knew it. We sang louder and louder. If I had not personally had been there to experience this, I would not have believed it myself. It was so magical to see the flames rise as our praises did. The flames looked like they were touching the stars. God's presence was so powerful that even though the bonfire was burning very brightly and powerfully enough to keep me warm, I had chills and goosebumps from the Holy Spirit in the atmosphere.

God took me back to *that* specific moment. I then realized this has happened before. Everything in the Bible repeats itself.

There is a story of a prophet named Elijah in 1 Kings 18. I will not write it out, but this is my main points paraphrase. Please, read the entire story on your own.

The people had abandoned the Lord's commands. They began to follow Baal (an idol). There were 450 "prophets" that worshiped and believed in the power of Baal. Elijah is upset because they are divided between Baal and God. He says to the people, "If the Lord is

God, follow Him; but if Baal is God, follow him." Elijah challenges the prophets. He tells them to get two bulls as sacrifices, one for Baal, one for God. He lets them choose the bull of their choice, set up their sacrifice, and tells them that the *real* God is a God of fire and that they should call to their god (Baal) to burn the sacrifice. The prophets call out to Baal for a long time, and nothing happened. Elijah mocks them because their god isn't answering them. Then, it is Elijah's turn to offer the sacrifice to the real God. He gathers up twelve stones, sets up the altar, cuts up the sacrifice, dedicates the offering to God. He then did something that was weird, as if all of this wasn't weird enough. He had the prophets fill up four large jars with water and had them pour the water on the offering and on the wood. Weird. Then, he commands them to do it a third time. Everything was drenched! He then, in verses 36–39:

> [...] stepped forward and prayed to the Lord, "God of Abraham, Issac, and Israel, let it be known today that you are God in Israel and that I am your servant and have done these things at your command. Answer me, Lord, answer me, so these people will know that you, Lord, are God, and that you are turning their hearts back again." Then the fire of the Lord fell and burned up the sacrifice, the

wood, the stones, and the soil. The people saw
this and were amazed and cried "The Lord—
he is God! The Lord—he is God!"

1 Kings 18:36–39 (NIV)

When you read the scripture in its entirety, the fire is
described as one so powerful that it even burned up the
soil. I wish I could have been there because when you
read commentary or look at images of what it would
have looked like back then, it makes you wonder how
high the flames were and how beautifully and powerfully God gloried Himself in the impossible. Although
my experience was not one as intense as the one of the
prophet Elijah, I was able to experience the glory and
power of God. Similarly, the wood was drenched, and
there was slim to none hope that it would burn. When
our praises raised, so did the flames. Now, I laugh at my
ignorance and unbelief. God has been faithful to fulfill
His promises since the beginning of time, and He *will*
glorify Himself because He is God. He alone has all the
power and glory forever and ever. He is with you, and
He has been with you from the very beginning. God
showed me His glory; how could I forget? I didn't know
I was about to walk into one of the hardest seasons of
my life.

If you're like me, you can be focused and distracted
by your circumstances and can miss God's glory in your

everyday life or even forget a moment when God revealed Himself to you. If this is you, say this prayer in agreement with me:

Lord, You are God! Thank You for everything that You have done in my life. Forgive me for feeling sorry for myself and, at times, do not trust in Your almighty power. Open my eyes, ears, and heart to be able to see, hear, and feel You in my life. I pray that Your voice is louder than any other voice in my life. Help me live a surrendered life trusting in Your love for me and that You cause all things to work for my good because I love You, and You have a purpose for me. Help me cling to Your promises because they are true, and You are faithful. In Jesus' name, amen.

CHAPTER 3

Playa del Nightmare

I arrived in Cancún by myself. I would be lying if I said I wasn't a little afraid that the driver taking me from the Cancún airport at midnight to the Riviera Maya would not kidnap me like in the movie *Taken*. I was playing all the worst-case scenarios in my head and coming up with an escape plan in case things did, in fact, take a wrong turn.

Traveling alone hadn't been in my plans. I purchased a trip for two, for four days, as a romantic getaway attempting to salvage a ticking time bomb of a relationship. I had planned everything down to perfection for optimal fun for our "romantic getaway."

The first day, I was at the resort the entire day by myself. I slept in, exercised, and had an extravagant breakfast. I wasn't in any hurry, since he wouldn't arrive until 10 p.m. I made my way to the beach with a few novels and absorbed the sun as the Caribbean waves serenaded me to a lovely siesta. I was in perfect peace. I thought to myself, *Do I really want him to arrive? We have been on and off in this relationship for a few years. We never get it right, but he is what I know.*

I made my way to the pool, and one of the servers brought me a piña colada. I was not much of a drinker, but hey, I was in paradise on vacation. The beverages kept coming, and I befriended a few internationals: Germans, to be exact.

One of my faults is that I have always been an overly trusting person. I did not know the Germans, but I thought them to be kind. The drinks kept coming even if I was not the one to order them. Most would consider that an obvious red flag.

I received a call that he would be arriving soon. I had lost track of time, and the swim-up bar was closing. The friends who I had made offered to walk me back to my room. My senses kicked in, and I declined their offer.

I was afraid because I was still alone. Every room and floor looked the same, and I stumbled as I tried to find my way. I wanted to cry because of the situation I found myself in. How did I get so lost? Figuratively and literally.

By the grace of God, I made it back to my room in time to evacuate my dinner through my mouth. I cried, sitting on the restroom floor. I remember so vividly wondering how I found myself in such a dark place, not just that night but progressively.

My contemplation didn't last long, as he was already waiting downstairs. I had to maneuver my way to the lobby to get him checked in. His reservation was lost, and the night manager of the resort was being anything but kind or accommodating. The night manager was basically saying that my boyfriend could not stay and that we would have to leave. In my current altered state, I was still able to think logically and call our travel agent. She made a few calls, and my boyfriend was given access and allowed to stay. He was upset and annoyed; somehow, the hotel problem was my fault, as things usually were.

I was extremely sick the following morning; I could not even take a sip of water without throwing up. I had no time to be sick, though. We had two excursions planned that day. Our bus would be picking us up shortly. He was already annoyed at breakfast; I didn't want to make matters worse.

Our commute to the Tulum ruins was about an hour, and there was no bathroom on the bus. I prayed to God to let me arrive in a restroom safely because I did not want to cause a scene. I was so humiliated, and I felt like such an inconvenience to him. It was extremely hot that day, and I was severely dehydrated. I could not drink water; my body would reject it. I was miserable, but I would not allow myself to show it. I wanted him to be happy. Thank God, we went to a cenote spring, and when I dove in, I felt a surge of energy and slight relief. Maybe the water was absorbing into my system; who knows?

The next couple of days were like that first one. Physically, I was better, but the trip was never-ending negative comments and bickering. The only time he was happy was when we went snorkeling. In that moment, I felt relief because at least he would take something positive from the trip. My happiness did not matter. My happiness came from his happiness.

Finally, it was time to depart, and when we arrived at the airport, there was no air conditioning or Internet. I know, I know: first world problems. I remember praying to God for things to stop going wrong because I could not handle the situation anymore. Matters got worse.

I was relieved when we boarded the plane because the air conditioner was blasting. I was exhausted and wanted nothing more than a nap. I leaned my head on his shoulder to use as my pillow. He shook me off. He said he was annoyed and did not feel like it.

What was left of my heart shattered in that moment. I did not ask him for anything, yet he did nothing but treat me poorly. I knew I wasn't perfect, but how long was I going to "pay" for forgiveness? How long was I going to pay for breaking his heart when I left for college?

When I left for college, I had trampled on this man's heart, with no regard for anyone's feelings but my own. Since then, I had worked to make amends, but it seemed like no matter what I did, I was still trying to earn his forgiveness.

I had booked this trip completely out of my own pocket. I was understanding that he was not making as much money as a teacher compared to an engineer. I accommodated his every need. I was not needy. I gave him his space and let him go "party" with his friends. I was the cool girlfriend who would welcome the girls his friends brought back to the house for an after-party. I moved back home in the middle of my master's program because he wanted me home to work on our relationship. I did not think about it twice and did it. After all that, I couldn't lean on his shoulder and rest my eyes after an exhausting trip?

My mom picked us up at the airport. I was past feeling sorry for myself. He could not be bothered to help lift the heavy luggage onto the vehicle. He just stood there and watched my mom and me struggle. When I dropped him off, I was ready to never see him again. I did not love this man, nor did he love me. The time spent together on and off meant nothing.

I sought guidance from my mom and aunt about my situation. They convinced me that it was normal in a relationship because everyone had their ups and downs. They shared that they had gone through similar. They encouraged me to be there for him and continue to support him. I listened. I did not see anything good in him, but they did, so I thought I must be wrong.

I repeatedly ignored all the signs to end the relationship and decided to stay based on well-intended advice, which was the wrong advice nevertheless. I convinced myself that I had sacrificed so much for this relationship that I had to make it work, even if it cost me my happiness.

A few days after our vacation, I started feeling anxious without an apparent reason. I felt that something was wrong. I was feeling more insecure than ever before but kept telling myself that I was the problem.

One day, I headed to work from his house. I had the keys to his house since I practically lived there. He was gone for most of the day. He had been short in his responses to my text messages. When I called him, he said that he was at his dad's shop working on a car. That was usually code for "I'm busy. Leave me alone," so I did. I started to feel sick this time.

I had dinner with a cousin of mine and ended it early because I needed to go home. I couldn't explain the nausea. I just knew something was not right. I called him to tell him that I was not feeling well and that I was going to bed early. He was still at his dad's shop and responded, "Okay." I fell asleep, but the anxious feeling didn't go away. I called him again; he didn't answer. I tossed and turned.

I received a message from a woman on Facebook. She asked me who I was. She had seen my name on his phone. She proceeded to tell me all the details about her relationship with him. That was the last day I saw him.

If you feel sorry for me, it is okay. Honestly, I sometimes mourn for that girl I used to be. She did not know how loved she is and how worthy she is of love. Even to this day, I sometimes start believing the lie that I am not worthy of love.

I know now that the life I was living before was dark and that God used this man to bring me back home. I thought this experience happened to me so that I could be with this person, but no, it was so that God could work in my heart. That was only the beginning. I would love to tell you that after this relationship, my eyes were opened, and I was wise about my relationships and went on to live happily ever after. That story is still being written; however, what I have found is better.

Crowning Moment

Finding out that I was worthy of love. Leaving when something is wrong is okay. I did not have to stay because it was what I knew.

Armor I Needed: Breastplate of Righteousness

By putting on the Breastplate of Righteousness, I put on the Righteousness of Jesus, which is Jesus; the more I put on Jesus, the more I become like Him. The more I become like Him, the less that sin, darkness, and confusion run my life.

Verse to Remember

"But now, this is what the Lord says—he who created you, Jacob, he who formed you, Israel: 'Do not fear, for I have redeemed you; I have summoned you by name; you are mine'" (Isaiah 43:1, NIV).

CHAPTER 4

The Heartbreak

I remember the first time I saw him. I noticed him immediately, but I looked the other way, so no one else would notice me looking at him. I thought: *Who is he? He must be a coach. Why else would he be here? He must be a middle school coach. They usually come around the week before their football season starts to learn from the high school coaches.*

I was standing by my gator with my students focused on the football practice when I felt him walking toward me. He proceeded to shake my hand and say, "Good morning, doc." He walked away. All I could say was, "Good morning, coach." I assumed that he was a coach. I didn't see him at practice the rest of the week.

I did not feel like Applebee's for Thirsty Thursday. I would tell myself that I needed to do things out of my comfort zone, even if it was hanging out with teacher co-workers that I did not know. The same man from practice arrived at our table. I don't know what it was about him, but I could not stop staring at him. Yes, it was creepy on my part. There was something about him. I was just drawn to him. He was quiet, yet everyone knew him.

The next morning, I still had early morning football practice. After practice, I made my way to the library to check out my computer for the upcoming school year. I was having a conversation with our librarian when out of the corner of my eye, I saw a man approaching the library. He was still far away, but immediately, I was attracted to him. He was tall, wearing slacks, a white collared shirt, dress shoes, and Oakley sunglasses. This man walked with such confidence; I couldn't look away. He walked in through the glass double doors.

As I saw him clearly, I noticed it was him. Ugh, I wanted to slap myself in the face. On three different occasions, I was drawn to this man, without knowing it was the same man. I was a bit thankful for that realization because if not, I would have felt that I was looking at every man with hungry eyes. Does that make sense?

He walked toward me, said hi to the librarian, and gave me a side hug. It was so awkward, primarily because of me. "I am sorry, I smell." Those were the words that vomited out of my mouth following the said hug. I said an equally awkward goodbye, thanked the librarian, and bolted back to my cave, where I clearly belonged.

I was barely making my way back to my office when my phone buzzed. It was him. From then on, we didn't stop talking. I made it evident that I liked him, but he was still acting oblivious to it all. I was the one doing the pursuing in this relationship. I noticed it was a common pattern in my life; I always felt that I needed to take control when it came to men.

We had been entertaining a flirtationship for about a month when my patience ran out, and in frustration, I confronted him, "Are you dumb? Can you really not tell that I like you and want to be with you?" He replied that he knew, which added even more to my frustration. I am part of that generation who needs the instant gratification. I want something, go for it, and get it. It is usually my way or the highway.

I noticed that even before the relationship officially began, I had already been begging this man for attention and affirmation that were not freely given. However, after that conversation with him, he completely changed. He started prioritizing me and treating me like his girlfriend. I justified to myself that the way I had acted was right because some men are shy, and maybe he had just needed that extra push. I assured myself that we all are afraid of rejection.

That relationship really did go from zero to one hundred real quick. I made him my whole entire life. I wanted to spend every single free second with him. I even left work to have lunch with him every day. I could not get enough of him; I became addicted to him.

It did not help that we were not living a God-honoring relationship. The number of times that he had stepped inside a church in his lifetime could probably be counted on the fingers of one hand.

Seeking God was also not number one on my priorities. I mean, I was a little "churchy." To me, what that meant was going to church for one hour every Sunday, checking it off from my to-do list, and continuing living in sin. I could do as I pleased because God is a God who loves and forgives. I knew God and had felt His presence, but I did not know Him through my actions. I was able to see, yet I was still blind. I was living my life the way I wanted to and would place God back on the shelf when the Bible did not agree with my actions. Sinning and repenting were all that I knew; they were all I had ever done.

I was okay with me being the only one in the relationship going to church because I was still learning. I was patient and trusted that he would come to church when God called him back. This was the type of relationship that I had with God. God was second in my life; this man was first.

Even though I had made my way back to church, would pray, and repent, I continued to sin. Yes, it is impossible to go a day and not sin, but when you are knowingly trying to better yourself and listening to convictions, it is a different story. What I mean by sinning is that I knew that I was intentionally making wrong decisions, and I was okay with my actions. I was focused on myself and what I wanted—nothing else.

What I wanted was to make this man happier than anyone else had ever made him. I knew that he had a difficult past and wanted to be the person to make it all better. It is funny because at this stage in my faith, I did not know anything other than Christ died for me, which should have been enough from the beginning, but I knew that logically and not emotionally. I did not know any better, and unfortunately, my spiritual leaders would focus on God's grace and not enough truth.

Why did I keep thinking that I could change men and make a difference in their lives? A person will not change unless they want to change. Think about how hard it is to change ourselves and to be disciplined to eat healthy, work out, read our Bible, and focus on our relationship with God. That change only happens when we want to change and take the necessary steps to work toward achieving that desired outcome.

My desire to be loved and wanted by my boyfriend was so big that I was exhausting myself trying to be the perfect girlfriend. When he would make comments about my physical body, I would obsess and spend hours at the gym and on treadmills fearing that if I gained weight, he would leave me. When he would comment on how he disliked my male friends because they were men, I completely shut those friendships out of my life for fear of losing him. I became isolated and lived only for him. He was all I saw and lived. He, however, kept me a secret.

How was I so blind to be okay with all of this? I complied with changing any behavior that he wanted me to change. He was slowly chipping away at the person I was and making me change into the woman he thought I should be. However, I fell short of his expectations every single time. He would make me feel ashamed of myself and like I was never enough. That feeling still creeps and tries to haunt me today. That lie is a lie that I take captive and submit to God daily. I thought I was in a healthy relationship. I loved him so much. I just wanted to be good enough for him. To the right person, you will not have to exhaust yourself physically and mentally to prove that you are enough because you are already enough.

The thing with emotional abuse is that it is subtle. You do not know that you are in an abusive relationship. I did not know that I was in an abusive relationship until five months post-breakup. It starts with minor changes that you start to make within yourself to make your significant other happy. You continue to make behavior modifications transforming you into someone else, and because this person has conditioned you a certain way, you believe that their actions toward you are because they love you. You keep justifying their behaviors and yours, and you start to believe the lies that keep being spoken over you.

Because I had isolated myself from my friends and family, I had no one to tell me that what I was doing was wrong. Nobody knew what I was going through. In my head, I was in the perfect relationship. I would mentally boast to myself about how lucky I was to have found this person to love me so well and because we never fought. The only times we did argue was when I did something "wrong" that he did not approve of. I saw no flaws in him and was desperately trying to be perfect for him to gain his approval, but we did not fight. I just submitted to his way of thinking. I did not know any better.

I wish I could go back and tell myself that was not love. I wish I could protect my younger self from the pain that she would later have to endure. We cannot travel back in time.

When we find ourselves in these kinds of situations, it is important to seek out the truth more and attempt to live in that truth. It is important that we surround ourselves with people who are grounded in biblical truth and seek their counsel. Finally, when we sin because we are not perfect beings, we can rest assured that God's grace is there for us, calling us home to Him.

Crowning Moment

Understanding and learning that the relationship I was in was abusive and not healthy.

Armor I Needed: Helmet of Salvation

A renewed mind and identity as a child of God who was already worthy and loved.

Verse to Remember

"We destroy arguments and every lofty opinion raised against the knowledge of God, and take every thought captive to obey Christ" (2 Corinthians 10:5, ESV).

CHAPTER 5

Rejection As Protection

I felt that I kept going through a similar cycle in my life with men. I could have sworn that after each relationship I was in, these men would then go on and marry the person they dated after me. That was extremely crushing and devastating. The feelings of rejection and unworthiness were always maximized in these moments.

Sometimes, the pain was so severe that I felt as if I had been tackled by a three-hundred-pound lineman, and then for the fun of it, he decided to sit on my chest. I could not physically breathe. I started noticing that in all the relationships that I had been in, it did not matter who ended the relationship; the men would eventually come back into my life and try to fix what was broken between us.

I would like to say that I always stood my ground and resisted the temptations to go back. That was not always the case. I learned the difficult way later that an apology without changed behavior means nothing.

This ex-boyfriend specifically was the most charismatic man that I had ever met. His words were sweeter than honey. I would mindlessly forgive him for stonewalling me (silent treatment) only to find myself in the same situation yet again. After multiple failed attempts at reconciliation, I would replay the entire relationship over and over in my mind and dissect when and where we went wrong. It was difficult for me to move on from this relationship.

Yet, he kept pursuing me. He would show up at my workplace, house, or any other places I frequented. It became a borderline Lifetime movie. He was genuinely apologetic, and I know he did want to make the relationship work. He just did not know how. For any relationship to work (advice from a single person), we must put our pride and anger aside and continue to care for our significant other. As the quote from John Mark Comer states, "Love is the decision of the will and of the heart to put another person's good ahead of your own. To sacrifice your good on the altar of another person's flourishing."

When I was dating this man, my relationship with God was unexclusive. My dates with God would only be on Sundays for an hour, and I would continue to do as I pleased the other six days of the week. I didn't know how much more there was or how much real love I was missing. I was constantly craving love—well, what I thought love was.

My desire to be loved was so immense that anytime my ex-boyfriend would show an ounce of love, I would grab at it and hold on to it with all my might. That ounce of love would sustain me the way a car runs after the gas light turns on. It would be only a matter of time before I was running on fumes. He was smart, though. Just before I would be completely on empty, he would give me another ounce of "love," and it would mean the world for me.

I would justify his behavior and mine. I would think to myself, *It's okay. I'm okay. He loves me so much. That is why he is so jealous. He has been through so much; he has been hurt before. I am so lucky to have someone who loves me this much and only wants me all to himself; it is such an honor. He is good. He has never hurt me. He has never called me names. I know other women who are in real abusive relationships. Their husbands demean them by calling them terrible names, sometimes in front of their children. Their husbands cheat on them, and they know it. They are so afraid to be alone that they are willing to put up with their unfaithfulness. That must be sad. Nope. Not me. I am the lucky one. He does not drink. He does not like to go out except to all-men barbeques. He doesn't have a spending problem. So, what if he is a little jealous?*

These were the false affirmations that I would repeat to myself in my head, comparing my relationship with other people's relationships. We had been in that vicious cycle of breaking up and getting back together. Every time we would break up again, he would take another chip of my heart, like a collector trying to gain my whole heart with no intentions of doing anything with it other than selfishly keeping it for himself.

I recently talked to my friend Jackie, actually semi-scolded her, "Why did you let me keep getting back together with him? You knew better; you saw what I couldn't see. I was so blinded. Why did you not stop me or tell me not to go back?" She replied, "What good would it have been for me to tell you not to do something? You were going to ultimately make your own choices. I could have told you not to get back together with him, but I was respecting your decision. I told you what I thought. I was ready to guide you toward the truth. You had to let God matter more and let him go all by yourself, through your own will."

Jackie was right. She loved me like Jesus loves us. In my struggle, she showed me kindness, grace, and so much patience. She knew how much I was hurting. She felt the pain I was feeling; I know this for a fact. Yet, she still let me choose my fate. Her heart was filled with so much compassion and empathy that every tear I cried, she cried with me. She did tell me the truth, even though it was not what I wanted to hear at times. Ultimately, my decisions were my own and came with their own set of consequences, but she loved me with grace and truth. Is it not so beautiful how God strategically places people in our lives to show us a glimpse of heaven?

Some time passed after this breakup, and one day, he showed up unexpectedly to have a few words. I had already made the decision to move on from him. He wanted to talk; I listened. He still sounded like a broken record. He didn't say anything different; he was being his charismatic self, attempting to manipulate me into believing his lies yet again. I had been praying about my situation with him. I can honestly say that it was divine intervention that I made it out of that toxicity.

Now, let me tell you about the best and worst moment of my life. After this breakup, I was so broken and lost that I ran full force to God. I was done with doing things my way. Everything up to that point in my life had been a failure, but then, I met Jesus. Jesus began to heal my heart. Little by little, He began to strategically place people in my life to minister to me, love me, and help me grow in my walk with Him. I attended a service at a new church one Wednesday in February that sparked something in me that made me hungry for God. I was so depressed that when I stepped into that church, I was finally at peace and didn't feel like crying. I was okay when I was at church, so I craved being at church to feel that same peace. Being at church 24/7 was not realistic, though, but I had a new desire.

That same weekend, I left on a work trip. I was on a charter bus with a team of soccer boys in Costa Rica. It was work, but every free opportunity I had, I would put on my headphones and blast worship music. It was literally the only thing that brought me peace since I couldn't be in an actual church. Thank you so much, Zach Williams, and your album *Chain Breaker*. God used you to minister to my life.

Listening to worship music was the only way that I could keep my composure; otherwise, I would cry. I could not understand why he had broken up with me, yet he still wanted to be in my life. I was so hurt and confused, but I loved him and thought some of him in my life was better than a life without him.

Like my friend Zandra says in her podcast *On the Way with Zandra*, "facts don't matter." It is all about shifting our perspective. What you focus on is what you will think.

In that moment, I was devastated. I was feeling alone, rejected, and crying for a man that did not want to be with me. I stared out the window, and I was looking at the actual rainforest. It was so beautiful. It had been raining all day; I thought I was causing the rain with my sadness (again, I know, selfish).

I was listening to a song, and the lyrics said, "What a beautiful name, the name of Jesus." I felt something in my heart, a nudge, but in that moment, something shifted. I rubbed my chest and checked my left arm, making sure I was not having a heart attack. I looked up again. The sky was still dark; it was still raining. In the far distance, there was an opening in the sky. The sun was shining through in the most beautiful, indescribable way.

The ray of sunshine was shining so bright on the rainforest in the distance, and I felt as if God was speaking to me: "I know you are hurting, daughter; I know you are in a storm now. It may seem dark and gloomy right now, but you can put your hope and trust in Me. The sun will shine again. The rain is necessary to wash everything that I did not have for you. You do not need to understand right now what I am doing. Be still. The sun will shine again."

I was so beautifully broken in that moment; I did not even attempt to hide the tears. I was getting weird looks from teenage boys, but nothing mattered more than being in the presence of God in that moment.

I did not know God well at this point in my life, yet He kept speaking to me through His creation and thoughts that I know were not mine, dreams, and other Christians. I used to think that I had to be made right and perfect before I could come to Him with my problems. God kept showing me that He loved me in my mess; I could come to Him whenever, and He was always there, hugging me and comforting me. I couldn't explain biblically at the time what was happening.

I just knew that God was with me, and He was making sure that I knew it was Him. I made the decision in that moment that I was going to give back. God had been so good to me. I had found myself extremely blessed in one of the most beautiful countries in an all-expense-paid trip as well as getting paid for my services. I apologized for being so selfish. I then decided to go on a mission trip.

That work trip ended. Because I was the designated grown-up, I was on the last flight back home. All the boys were flying to different parts of the United States, so I was to ensure they boarded their flights. This meant an extreme layover in Houston.

I began to Google-search mission trips. I came across a website called Adventures in Missions. I was looking at all their missions, locations, and times. I was excited because they offered trips that were also on my travel bucket list. I thought I could, in a way, double-dip. It made sense: travel and ministry—how cool! I actually didn't know what ministry was at this point; I just felt that I had to follow this "lead" that God was giving me.

During the wait time, I made a few phone calls, and one of my friends told me that the church I had visited had mission trips for the summer. I thought to myself, *I would rather go on a mission trip with local people than complete strangers.* I looked up the mission trips for my local church. They were offering four different trips to Costa

Rica. I will confess: I immediately thought, *No, not there, I just came back from there.* Just then, I felt a tug in my heart, and I smirked and looked up at God and said, "Okay, God, I get it."

The next day, I went to a mid-week service and signed up for a summer mission trip. They informed me that the trip was full but that they would keep my application and call me if anyone canceled. I prayed and left it in God's hands. The very next day, I received a call from one of the staff pastors, and he told me that someone had just canceled. I smiled again; I already knew God was going to do it. This trip was the start of something new.

In the weeks prior to the trip, there were preparation meetings. We gathered as a group and got to know each other a little better. We began praying for each other, and God blessed me with Jackie as a support system. I was getting mentally and spiritually ready for that trip.

The night before we were to leave, he showed up at my doorstep. I called Jackie immediately and asked her to pray. I needed reinforcements. This man had a way of talking, though. He said all the right things and had me questioning my decision. He had a way of speaking that I would often find myself apologizing for things that I did not even think or do. I thought maybe God was blessing me because I had been seeking Him (God), and maybe He would bring us back together. He brought me an umbrella because he knew I did not have one, and well, the rainforest is rainy. It was sweet. I went on the trip excited and full of hope of a relationship resurrection because Jesus could do it.

Two days into the trip, he stonewalled me because he remembered something that made him upset. It was somehow my fault (I didn't realize at the time that I had patterns and tendencies to be attracted to a certain type of man). When we were dating, we never fought—maybe because I was always trying to be perfect and never upset him.

When I began walking with God, God gave me strength, boldness, and confidence, which threatened him, so he would get upset and shut me out. It was my punishment for not acting according to his desires. It would work before, but God had just begun a new work in me. God was holding my hand, guiding my broken heart out of the darkness. We didn't speak for the rest of the trip, but I know it was God. God's love kept breaking through the hardened walls of my heart. I experienced so much on that trip, and I was full. That trip is a book by itself.

I thought after I had received so much from God and that trip that there was no way I was going to go back to him again. However, I was still stubborn and, in fact, went back to him a couple of times. Each time I would spend time with him, I would feel pain, anxiety, and ironically lonelier than before. He didn't feel like home anymore, and I was constantly uncomfortable. I kept screaming to myself, "Stop fighting with God!"

I loved him, but I knew I had to let him go. God had clearly shown me repeatedly that it was over with him and that He had a different plan for me. There was a disconnect between my mind and my heart. I was battling with what I wanted and what I knew was right. My mind was made up, and I would be lying if I said it was easy. I was actively hiding from him and crying each time I ignored one of his calls. I had communicated to him that God had saved me and that I didn't want to live the same way as before. I had made the decision to follow Christ, and that required me saying goodbye to my past.

The tighter I clung to God, the harder my ex-boyfriend would pursue me. This situation would cause me physical pain to say no to him. The messages kept coming, and he then asked to meet up to exchange the belongings that we had of each other. I figured it was the right thing to do. He lived less than five minutes from my work. I could go and make a quick stop. As I was driving, I began to feel sick because I was nervous.

I prayed: "God, I need You right now. I am choosing to follow You over him. You know my heart, and You know I am weak. Help me in this conversation, Lord. Please, do not let me fall for his charm, and please, do not let him hurt my heart. I don't think my heart can break anymore. Amen."

I arrived at his house. He was sitting outside. I could tell he had been there for a while, thinking. His brother's car was parked in the driveway. There wasn't anywhere for me to park. He walked up to my window and stayed quiet. What was weirder was that I stayed quiet too. I handed him the rainforest umbrella, and since he didn't say anything, I assumed the interaction was over. I put the car in reverse and started driving away. I was getting to the end of the neighborhood when my phone vibrated. I smiled and thought, *That was weird. I am going to go back.* I looked at the message, and it read, "I was wrong. You're worthless."

What happened next is what my friend Jonathan would call a "nexus" moment. I will leave the definition up to Google. I made a left turn out of his neighborhood. I was crying uncontrollably, gasping, and holding on to the steering wheel as hard as I could. I pulled over because if I kept driving, I would have crashed. I was crying, but the tears were not out of sadness.

In the very same moment that I read that message that had all the power to destroy me, God met me. In that very same moment, I felt as if the heavens had opened, and God Himself descended and was embracing me in an inexplicable way. His presence was so powerful. All I could feel was immense love. I did not hear Him say this, but I felt Him say to me: "That is a lie, daughter. You are not worthless. You are worthy. I love you so much I sent My Son to die for you. Do not believe the lie. I am here with you. I love you."

I was crying and laughing, broken yet completely full. Everything made sense, yet it didn't. I had to take more than a few moments to gather myself together. I couldn't wrap my mind around what had just occurred. Then, I broke down again because I remembered my prayer. I had asked God to protect my heart. I had asked Him to help me with that interaction and give me strength because every time I spoke with this man, I would lose. God made it so that we didn't speak to each other.

I was about to turn around and head back to talk to my ex-boyfriend. I had felt guilty and rude, but this man texted me the one word that would guarantee that I would not go back. The word that should have crushed me: worthless. I know it was God. Let me explain.

This situation reminded me of the Israelites when they were enslaved in Egypt by Pharaoh. I won't go into the full detail of Scripture, but here is my synopsis. I repeat: my synopsis. Don't call the Bible police, okay? Thanks.

The Israelites were being treated horribly by Pharaoh. God had favor over them. Pharaoh saw that there were so many of them and was afraid they would overcome Egypt, so he made them labor and labor and labor. He would not let them worship God. God used Moses to speak and warn Pharaoh, but Pharaoh did not listen. God sent plagues over Egypt. The plagues were:

1. Water to blood (Exodus 7:14–25)
2. Frogs (Exodus 7:26–8:11)
3. Gnats (Exodus 8:12–15)
4. Flies (Exodus 8:16–28)
5. Disease of livestock (Exodus 9:1–7)
6. Unhealable boils (Exodus 9:8–12)
7. Hail and fire (Exodus 9:13–35)
8. Locusts (Exodus 10:1–20)
9. Darkness (Exodus 10:21–29)
10. Death of first born (Exodus 11:1–12:36)

Horrible, I know. Pharaoh would ask Moses to plead with God to make the plagues stop. He would promise to free the Israelites but would reverse his decision when the plagues were lifted. God hardened his heart each time. I was always confused about why God would harden Pharaoh's heart. Eventually, I realized that Pharaoh had many chances to do the right thing but kept doing what he wanted.

There are two types of people in the world: with God or against God. It is black and white. There is no gray or in-between. God is sovereign. His will forever will be done. God knows everything, and He knew that the Israelites were prone to looking back. After the last plague, Pharaoh was so broken because of the death of his son he told the Israelites to leave. The Israelites crossed the Red Sea. God hardened Pharaoh's heart, thus resulting in Pharaoh sending all his men, chariots, and resources after the Israelites. After the Israelites crossed the Red Sea, God released the waters and consumed Pharaoh and all the Egyptians with him.

God had the victory. If God had not hardened Pharaoh's heart, Pharaoh would not have been viciously chasing after the Israelites. Knowing what we now know about the nature of the Israelites, we can infer that Israelites would have probably made excuses to stay and justify that Pharaoh was not that bad when in fact, they were literally enslaved. To me, this tells me the following: God loves us so much that He does not want to leave us where we are.

If God had not hardened this man's heart and led him to say the words that would ensure that I would not go back, I would not have moved. I would have stayed, justified, and suffered in silence. For the Israelites, it was fear. For me, it was heartbreak that led to surrender. I am thankful for that heartbreak. Both were divine interruptions. If not for God, we would not have moved.

Narratives in the Bible are there so we can learn from their mistakes, specifically what not to do. The importance of learning history helps us not to repeat it. Yet, so many people (including me) ignore red flags and common sense. I would encourage you not to wait until your slavery, whether physical or emotional, is at the end-all, be-all stage. We don't have to wait until we physically see the flames to exit a burning building. We can leave at the first sign of smoke.

I learned that God is so loving and merciful, and He will never stop pursuing us, nor will He run out of grace. How many times are we going to go through the same heartbreak until we learn our patterns and do something about them? *How many times, Andrea?*

My ex-boyfriend was not a bad person; I was not perfect either. We were just two broken people with baggage and insecurities that were projecting them onto each other. I had made him my god and idol. Nothing and no one can fulfill you like God's love can. God's love for me was so much greater than my fear of being alone. This time, God had grabbed me firmly by my hand and did not let go. I understood that I needed to trust that my Father knew what was better for me. As the Word of God says in Jeremiah 29:11 (NIV): "'For I know that plans I have for you,' declares the Lord, 'plans to prosper you and not to harm you, plans to give you hope and a future.'"

I made the decision to move forward in faith, even if it meant falling on my knees in surrender, crying out to God, and believing that He can and will take my pain away. I had faith, and that faith required action. It was not a blindly optimistic faith that God would change him and reunite us; it was a faith that said: *You matter more. I want what you want. I believe you are who you say you are.*

Amid my deepest pain, I was able to experience God's immense love for me. It was a love like I had never experienced before. I had felt foolish for expecting any man to love me this way. It is physically impossible. Once I knew this, there was no going back. Believe me: I tried. I admit this embarrassingly.

A few months after that conversation with my ex-boyfriend and life-changing moment with God, my ex-boyfriend went to my office to talk to me again. My heart was racing, and I was trying to keep calm. He came to tell me about her. I already knew. He cleared his throat, looked down at my desk, and began to speak, "I want to tell you something. I want it to come from me before you hear it from anyone else. I am dating someone. She works here."

At this moment, I could have sworn that my heart dropped to my feet. Stabbing me in the heart would have probably been less painful. Even though I had made the choice to honor God in the decision not to go back to this relationship, I still loved this man. The news crushed me. I tried to keep my composure in the conversation. I opened my mouth to speak, "Thank you for telling me. Do I know her?" He replied, "No, but she knows you." The next thing he said to me practically killed me, "She goes to your church. I go with her; we go together. I wanted to tell you in case we run into you. I don't want you to be caught off guard. I don't want to hurt you."

I was struggling to hold back the tears and just kept thinking, Jesus, *help me, give me the words*. I felt a peace come over me and said, "I am happy that you are going to church. I am happy that you are seeking God and growing in your faith. Please, continue to go. Do not get discouraged because you might see me there. I am okay. Please, treat her right, respect her, and stop looking for me. Love her like you couldn't love me."

I wanted everything with this man, but I trusted that God's plan for my life was greater. I could have focused on why God did not change his heart and made him go to church with me, but God was showing me that I needed to fix my relationship with Him first. I kept thinking, *If I can love the wrong man this much, I can only imagine loving the one who God has for me, but even if He does not bring that person to my life, I want to know and believe that God is enough for me. That is the kind of love that will last forever.*

At this point in my life, I was new to walking with God. I still saw Him somewhat as a God that could grant me wishes like a genie. I was only beginning to microscopically understand what His love for me was.

Crowning Moment

God loves us so much that He does not want to leave us where we are.

Armor of Choice: Shield of Faith

My faith had to be bigger than my circumstance. I had faith that God had a better plan for me, even if I couldn't see it.

Verse to Remember

"'For I know that plans I have for you,' declares the Lord, 'plans to prosper you and not to harm you, plans to give you hope and a future'" (Jeremiah 29:11, NIV).

CHAPTER 6

The Girl With the Rose(s) Tattoo

Even though I was presenting with the symptoms of depression, it never crossed my mind that, in fact, I was depressed. I was able to function pretty well: I would go to work, do what I needed to, exercise, then go to sleep. I didn't talk to anyone, really. I wanted to work away the sadness. Life didn't stop because my heart was broken. I was getting thinner because, for the first time in my life, I didn't have an appetite for food. I didn't care; nothing mattered. I was smiling, though; I knew how to hide my depression well. Only my parents would see what I would do the second I got home, which was sleep. They never said anything; I think they didn't understand and didn't know what to say that would help. Honestly, I don't know what they could have said that would have helped. I was in a deep dark hole and didn't let anyone help me out. I prayed for God to take me "home," but He wasn't interested in answering that prayer. I knew logically what was happening, but I couldn't disconnect logic from my emotions, so I rode my emotions like the tidal wave that they were. I went over every single text message, every picture, every interaction in my mind to see if I could figure out when and where I went wrong. *Why would God hurt me this way?* I thought. People say that time heals all wounds; if you said this to me, I probably wanted to throw a heavy object at you. How could you possibly know what I was feeling? I didn't need clichés; I needed not to feel. I desperately wanted to self-destruct, but even then, God had a hold on me. Even in my circumstance, I was still able to stay away from substances; I was still paying the consequences of a DWI from college. I would have never thought that incident was a blessing in disguise. At least no one was hurt, and I had learned that lesson. I wanted to self-medicate, but I didn't know how or with what.

The gym became my drug, exercise in general. I remembered that *Legally Blonde* quote, "Exercise gives you endorphins; endorphins make you happy; happy people just don't kill their husbands." I was exercising every chance that I got. Exercise wasn't making me happy, but I began to like the results in my physical body. Then it hit me: I was going to work out, look amazing, and he'll want me back for sure. I had a new goal, a new focus. I had a new drive for exercising, so my physical body was feeling better, but my heart was still shattered. I didn't want to feel sad anymore. I wanted to feel anything but that. I would listen to hours and hours of sermons, and while they helped me understand God better, I couldn't rush this process as much as I wanted to. The Word was doing something, though, I couldn't explain it at the time, but I knew that God was working.

Joy and happiness were out of the question; I couldn't even channel a fake smile to a real smile, and I couldn't "fake it til you make it" anymore. I wanted to feel something other than sadness. I was still looking for another outlet. Then, the lightbulb turned on in my mind. I already had a black rose tattoo; why not add a red one? I had gotten the black rose when I was in a darker moment in life B.C. (Before Christ). I had been so lost in worldly things, and I felt as if a darkness was constantly following me around. I loved roses; I always have. I figured not many people had a "black" rose tattoo. When I was researching meanings of the different colors, the black one was the one I related to.

Google explanation: since black roses are impossible in nature, tattooing a black rose to yourself means you pursue the impossible. You hope for some kind of miracle, be it a reunion or love or journey.

That was true; I was believing in the impossible, that I would *feel* love again. To me, my black rose meant hope. A black rose is still beautiful and blooming despite the darkness. I had hope in the darkness before I knew God, and I had hope in this situation too. Now I am sharing my story, and I don't believe that we should go through extremes; this was just my experience.

Time had passed, and I'd forgotten how much a tattoo hurt. This time was different; I had real hope. I knew it would be painful, but I knew that I wouldn't be the same by the time this tattoo healed. I am not condoning tattoos, nor am I against them biblically (obviously), but that was and is my last tattoo that I will ever get. I wanted to feel something, and I did. My red rose to me meant that I believed that I would feel again, love again, and I did; I found that love in Jesus.

Crowning Moment

Feeling again.

Armor of God: Shield of Faith

When all seemed dark, I had faith that this darkness wouldn't be forever. I had hope.

Verse to Remember

"May the God of hope fill you with all joy and peace in believing, so that by the power of the Holy Spirit you may abound in hope" (Romans 15:13, ESV).

CHAPTER 7

Pay Attention: You Might Miss It If You Blink!

Breakups are never easy. It even says it in the Word: you are breaking something, a relationship. In a way, you are becoming broken. I have had my fair share of breakups, if you have not been able to tell by now. I would like to say that I have learned and gotten used to the process or the pain, but that is not true.

I am no parent, but I often hear parents who have more than one child talk about how different their children's needs are and how parenting is not a one-size-fits-all. This makes sense because we were all created to be different, with different needs varying from emotional, physical, and spiritual needs.

Yes, I will be biased and say that we all need Jesus, but that is probably a given, seeing as I am writing about how good God has been to me. To me, the process of going through a breakup is similar to what I think it is like is to that of having multiple children. There are some basic needs, dos, and don'ts that we go through. Ultimately, the growing (or, in this case, grieving process) will be different. Adjustments must be made to the needs of each specific relationship.

For as far back I can recall in my life, I have always been the person to "stay strong," meaning I do not love to show my vulnerability to others. When someone needed to be comforted, I was there, even at a young age. When my mom was devastated because my father left, not once did she see me cry. I was the one to literally wipe her tears and cheer her up. I had to be strong at eleven years old. I could not add to the breaking of my family. We were already broken.

When I had meniscus surgery, I went back to work the same day to show my students that pain was subjective and that we were as strong as we chose to be. I did not want to seem weak or vulnerable. I would secretly love when my friends would brag to others about me saying I was not human because I did not feel pain. I know they were talking about physical pain, but that statement took root in my heart. I would come back at it and think to myself, *Is there something wrong with me? Why am I numb?* I knew on the inside that I did have feelings and felt pain, but I never wanted people to see that side of me. I felt that my feelings would be an inconvenience to others and did not want to bother anyone with my pain.

I was the same way in my relationship with God. I would pray for physical and emotional healing for others but never wanted to bother God with my selfish, undeserving self. I don't know why it was so hard for me to show pain and sadness. They are both very real, raw, and beautiful emotions. Why was I trying to hide my pain and tears as if I was ashamed like Adam and Eve were in the garden?

God knows all of us, and He knows what we need. When it comes to coping with heartbreak, I turn to my coping strategies. They are:

- All of the Jesus I can get through, in the form of worship music, podcasts, books, and of course, church and community.
- Exercise and not extra fries. I must admit, though, that the fries will always be more tempting.
- Deleting all pictures on social media and phone. (This is hard because you remember the good moments.)
- Lastly, for me, keeping it together.

I try to go through my process and think that by just doing the previous things mentioned, I will deal with my heartbreak, and I will move on. Our hearts are not so simple, and emotions are far too real. I thought that the more I pretended to be okay in front of others, I eventually would be okay. I had the fake-it-until-you-make-it mentality. The beauty in the heartbreak that I was going through was that in my deepest pain and sorrow, that is the closest that I have ever felt the presence of God.

When my ex-boyfriend ended the relationship, I was devastated. It was unexpected, and I couldn't understand how he just stopped loving me. He went from saying he loved me one day to "I do not want to be with you" the next. I was rejected, unloved, and unwanted. It would take all the strength in me to keep it together at work in front of my coworkers and students. I would focus on my work and not let even a teeny tiny thought escape because it would be about him, and I would lose it and fall apart.

I would step into my car, put on my oversized sunglasses, wave goodbye to the security officer, and head to lunch. As soon as I made the right turn away from my campus, the tears would start falling automatically. There was no effort involved. I would keep it together. Once I was alone in the safety of my little Chevy Sonic with super dark but legally tinted windows, I was free to let go. The song "Oh My Soul" by Casting Crowns ministered to my life. I would listen to that song in the car during my crying sessions, and it felt as if God was singing those exact words to me:

"Oh, my soul,
Oh, how you worry,
Oh, how you're weary, from fearing you lost control
This was the one thing, you didn't see coming
And no one would blame you, though
If you cried in private
If you tried to hide it away, so no one knows
No one will see, if you stop believing
Oh, my Soul,
You are not alone
There's a place where fear has to face the God
You know
One more day, He will make a way
Let Him show you how, you can lay this down
'Cause you're not alone."[2]

Now hear me out. It may sound weird. I am not necessarily saying that I want to be in that place of hurt and pain again, but today, I can hear that same song, smile, look up, and reflect on how God was always with me. I did not really appreciate God's love for being there. I was focused on my hurt. God could have so easily rolled

---

2 Casting Crowns, "Oh My Soul," track 4 on The Very Next Thing, Provident Label Group LLC, 2016.

His eyes and laughed because He knew what He had for me in the future. I could not look past my pain and disappointment, yet God was *still* there mourning with me. Jesus mourned with Mary and Martha when Lazarus died. He knew He was going to come back. He knew with His whole heart that God was faithful and a keeper of His promises. He still cried out to God, and you can, too. God listens. He is always there. He is always speaking to us. We just have to listen carefully to His loving whisper.

Crowning Moment

When I lost what was everything to me, God showed me He was always there and that I was never alone.

Armor of Choice: Sword of the Spirit (The Word of God)

The Bible to know the truth and meditate on it. Use the truth to fight forward through life and circumstances; it is God's promise to us.

Verse to Remember

"This Book of the Law shall not depart from your mouth, but you shall meditate on it day and night, so that you may be careful to do according to all that is written in it. For then you will make your way prosperous, and then you will have good success" (Joshua 1:8, ESV).

CHAPTER 8

Her

I do not know why her presence bothered me. I have nothing against this woman. She didn't do anything to me; she just exists. Every time I see her, I compare myself to her. I wish I didn't, but like everything else, comparison is a choice.

When temptation comes knocking at our hearts and minds, we should strive to be like Joseph when he ran away from Potiphar's wife after she tried to seduce him. No, this woman was not seducing me; calm down, people. However, having negative and resentful thoughts about her was so very enticing, and envy seeds were being planted.

The thing is, we know the patterns. The enemy is not creative in the ways he attacks us. He uses the same methods repeatedly. How strong we are spiritually in those moments is ultimately what determines how we react in those situations. There have been many times when I recognize the patterns and know that the feelings and thoughts are not from God, and I can laugh and joke, "Nice try, Satan; not today!"

Other times, usually when I am tired and pulling away from some spiritual practices, I am not as wise to recognize these attacks. I begin comparing, judging, and condemning others in my mind. Those are all things that we are always warned against. The thoughts start off seemingly innocent. They seem subtle or harmless even. Sometimes, the enemy whispers to us in our own voice, which makes it easy to confuse as our own thoughts. That is why when we have these thoughts or feelings, we should have our plan of attack. Ephesians 6 says we are to put on the armor of God.

Let us face it. We are all human and do not always have the purest of thoughts. We judge people and do not think nicely of them when they hurt us or do not agree with us. Sometimes, it even feels good to feel superior; it is wrong, though. Am I superior? Of course not, but the prideful part of me sure likes to think so. We aren't to compare ourselves with others; each of us is fearfully and wonderfully made. Comparison is a thief of joy. I don't know if it is listed biblically as a sin, but I know if left unchecked, it leads to envy in my life.

For whatever reason, what my microscopic mind could not comprehend was that God had placed me at that season for a purpose. It is extremely hard not to fall into the trap of comparison when someone else has the happiness that you used to have. *That would have been me a few months ago. I was supposed to get the ring, marry him, and have that baby.* Those were my thoughts. Happiness is circumstantial. Joy, however, comes from within. Joy is a command, not a feeling. As the Word of God says in 1 Thessalonians 5:16–18 (NIV): "Rejoice always, pray continually, give thanks in all circumstances: for this is God's will for you in Christ Jesus."

I thought to God, *Wait. You are telling me to give thanks for the other woman, to pray for her and for me, and to be happy about it?* God said to me, "Yes!"

One Thursday evening at Corner Bakery Café, Priscilla slammed her hands on the table in frustration and exclaimed, "Why does my mood depend on my circumstances?" A common misconception is that once you accept Christ as your Savior, you are transformed. I hate to be the person to tell you this, but it does not happen like this. It is a process. We have only just begun the process of living a Christian life, trying to be like Jesus. I have some good days and some terrible days. I do know that through these trials and circumstances, God is working in me.

I remember how I would have hissy fits with God because both individuals worked with me. I would ask, *Why is he here, God? Why do I have to keep seeing him? Why do I have to see her?* I would pray and pray for my situation to be easier. I would constantly call Jackie, my lifeline through this breakup, for wisdom and the plain hard truth. She made a statement to me that blew my mind. She said, "Maybe God is allowing them to be in your life as a reminder of the life you could have had. You could have gotten back together with him. You chose God over him; God may be reminding you of that choice."

I wanted to cry then and there, but I was at work, so I choked back my tears. I was praying so hard for God to change my circumstances when all along, He was trying to change my heart. I was relying on my own strength to deal with my pain, problems, and insecurities. God wanted me to surrender those insecurities to Him when all I wanted was to control the outcomes of my circumstances. I was trying to be God.

My struggle with comparison was very real that it even became toxic for my life. If I was in the presence of someone talking about her, I would stay and listen to gossip because it made me feel better about myself. I felt like Cady Heron from Mean Girls when she was obsessed with Regina George. Talking about her and comparing myself would sometimes calm my insecurities for a while, but then, the envious thoughts would come back again. I started to realize that the thoughts were not even attacks against her. They were against me.

It took an honest assessment of my heart to understand why I was having these thoughts about this woman: *Why her? Is she better than me? Is she prettier? Does she* love him in a way I could not? Why was I not good enough? Was I not worthy? Why does she get the good parts of him when I loved him as hard as I could? Did he not see how much I loved him? I humiliated myself for him. She would probably never do that. She probably calls the shots. She knows her worth and demands to be treated with respect. Why didn't I? Why did he keep me a secret? Why did he so proudly claim her?

Friends, those thoughts were so poisonous to my life. I became so bitter. We can choose to dwell in the bad or the good. The way we look at our circumstances determines how we will live or die spiritually. I could have been focusing on the goodness of God for allowing me to walk away from that relationship unharmed. I do not even want to imagine what could have been, the person I would have become, or how far away I would be from my Father if I had stayed in that relationship. No, thank you.

When I would fight these thoughts about this woman that I know nothing about, I was battling the wrong person. I still have those thoughts that try to creep in occasionally, but I take them captive and make them obedient to Jesus Christ. I pray for them now, for their relationship, for spiritual growth, and for blessings. God loves them just like He loves me.

Anything that opposes the word of God is not from God. When these thoughts come into your mind, take control and send them back to where they came from.

Crowning Moment

Knowing that God made me fearfully and wonderfully made. What is for me is for me. No one can take a blessing that God has for me. My identity is in Christ and not in my appearances or relationships.

Armor of Choice: Helmet of Salvation
(The Mind of Christ)

When I am reminded of my salvation and of the sacrifice of Jesus dying on the cross for me because He loves me, all other love is incomparable.

Verse to Remember

"We destroy arguments and every lofty opinion raised against the knowledge of God, and take every thought captive to obey Christ" (2 Corinthians 10:5, ESV).

CHAPTER 9

Look, Dad!
No Hands!

The more I got to know God as my Lord and Savior, the more I fell in love. If we love Him truly, we will obey His commandments. You see, non-believers look at Christianity as some boring cult with so many rules and regulations. I discovered that it is the complete opposite. Once I experienced what Christianity was really like, it just made sense. I saw how much I was loved and why Jesus died on the cross for me. The answer was love in the purest of ways. I know there is no one that will ever love me in that way here on Earth, and it is okay. That kind of love is literally out of this world. The good news is that we do not have to be out of the world to experience it.

I started to see the relationship with my Father God like any other father-daughter relationship. I personally did not grow up with the best father figure, and perhaps many reading this have a similar situation. I love my dad, but I had to learn how to love my Heavenly Father to understand my earthly one.

When I was younger, my family and I lived in a mobile home in a retirement community. My parents and our neighbors had gotten special permission to be able to reside in this elderly community. There were not many neighborhood kids playing around.

One of the things that I love about my dad is that he always worked tirelessly to provide for our family. He would arrive home from work and still make time to spend with us. His goal at the time was to get me to learn how to ride my bike without any training wheels. I still remember vividly the day I learned to ride my bike. My dad was so patient in teaching me. As much as I tried to learn for him, I just could not get it and kept falling over. I was thankful for the helmet and knee pads.

One afternoon, while my dad was still at work, the neighborhood kids (all two of them) and I were determined to have me ride my bike without training wheels. I kept falling. I was frustrated and discouraged. I kept thinking of how I wanted to make my dad proud; I didn't want to disappoint him.

A couple of Winter Texans who lived there saw my many failed attempts and approached us. The man said that he saw that I had fallen a few times (that was modest of him), but he liked how I kept getting up. I didn't care so much for the compliment at the time because I was frustrated at the memory of me falling repeatedly. He then made a wager with me. He said that he and his wife were going to walk for a bit but that if I learned to ride my bike in the meantime, he would give me $10. (This was in the '90s, so at the time, it was a sweet gesture; in the present day, it would be a *Criminal Minds* episode.) I agreed. My friends and I kept practicing.

Before my dad got home that evening, I was riding my bike up and down the street with no training wheels and even no hands for a few seconds. I still remember the smile on my dad's face as he drove in that old champagne-colored Malibu. When I think back to this moment, I still recall that feeling of happiness that I felt from making him proud. My ability to ride a bike had no added benefit to my dad's life. He was simply proud of what I had accomplished. I never saw the Winter Texan again, nor did I receive those highly motivating ten dollars.

In my head, that is how our relationship with God, our Father, should be. It is not just rules and laws to follow so that we make it to heaven. He is a Father who cares about us and wants us to grow up from being a little girl/boy who scrapes her/his knees to become the beautiful young woman/man He created us to be. The first commandment is to love God, as stated in Mark 12:30 (NIV): "Love the Lord your God with all your heart and with all your soul and with all your mind and with all your strength."

We should want to live a life that makes Him smile back at us. After all, He created us to glorify Him. When you live life free, as we all should, our actions become actions of love. We should be obedient out of love, not because someone told us to. I repeat 1 John 4:19 (NIV): "We love because He first loved us first." He cares about us so much that even when things do not go the way we want, we know that it is because He has something better for us. Like a father loves his child, God loves you and me and wants His best for us.

I would love to tell you that because I know the truth, I am immune to the attacks of the enemy. Obviously, I am not. I have met so many people through my church and community. It is crazy to think that everyone has a pain or struggle that they face daily. I would see these people and think to myself, *I want what they have, they are so happy, they have the perfect lives. If I accept Jesus, then I won't have problems, and I will be happy just like them.* Let's all take a moment and laugh at my ignorance. It is okay if you thought this too; I won't tell.

I soon found out two things. Number one being that everyone who is Christian has gone through so much. Number two, *everyone* who is *not* a Christian has gone through so much. Do I believe that you can have a successful, fulfilling life without knowing Christ? The answer is of course, depending on how you measure success. There are non-believers that the world considers successful and that I still admire who have endured through and through, and they are okay.

The difference, which in my opinion is the most important factor, is Jesus. I do not mean this to sound whiney or high school (in my defense, I worked at one), but when I hear a believer's testimony, and they are vulnerable to share their pain and ways of persevering, I think to myself, *I am not okay, but it is okay. If they made it out of that darkness, then so can I.* I am so thankful that God placed people in my life that had gone through similar trials and persevered. Their advice and wisdom were not a generic one-size-fits-all type of advice; it was real because they had gone through the storms themselves. They offered real "me too" moments and were there to comfort me.

When I look back on all that I have been through, I see that there is good in the pain because I can now use that experience and knowledge to help others just like others helped me. God works in us so that He can work through us. We are brothers and sisters, after all, and must look out for each other.

We are a family, the body of Christ, trying to live a life that is pleasing to our Father. I picture God smiling at us when we use our gifts, talents, and experiences to build each other up.

Crowning Moment

God loves me, and there is nothing I have to do to earn His love. His love is freely given because He created me to love me.

Armor of Choice: Breastplate of Righteousness (The Righteousness of Christ Jesus)

To be Christlike in the way I love and treat others. WWJD?

Verse to Remember

"Praise be to the God and Father of our Lord Jesus Christ, the father of compassion and the God of all comfort, who comforts us in all our troubles, so that we can comfort those in any trouble with the comfort we ourselves receive from God" (2 Corinthians 1:3–4, ESV).

CHAPTER 10

Spiritual Cardio

I hate cardio. "Cardio is hardio" is usually the caption that I write on my post-workout sweaty Instagram selfie. I know hate is a strong and negative word, but I want to make a point on how much I dislike it.

My daily routine consists of me waking up at 4:15 a.m. to make myself either run or make it to the gym for my daily exercise regimen before getting to work at 6:30 a.m. My love of food makes me want to be consistent with exercise. Of course, there are other benefits such as stress relief, health, etcetera...I have personally seen the positive benefits that exercise has on my life; I have seen the detrimental ones when I do not.

The benefits of health from exercise in my life usually outweigh the lazy thoughts that creep up before I make the decision to get out of bed and go exercise. Exercise has become a part of my lifestyle that usually comes naturally to me; the going part I still struggle with physically. I noticed that the more I show up, the more I want to keep going to see my progress. I have off-days when I just go, walk on the treadmill for a few minutes, and then sneak out to the sauna. Those days are still very therapeutic. We cannot be *on* all the time.

I crushed my friend Jackie's feelings the other day. I can't recall the exact phone conversations, but it was something along the lines of "Okay, Jack; I have to hang up. I have to wake up early tomorrow to go work out. Ugh, I hate working out." I don't know if this is possible, but I am pretty sure I heard her jaw drop. For as long as we had known each other, she has seen me as her "fit" friend. I felt like I had just revealed to a child that Santa Claus was not real. I then proceeded to tell her how every day, I must actively make the choice to go exercise. Yes, some days, it is effortless. Other days, I am battling myself in my mind and physically slapping myself to get up and go. The thing is, I never regret going to the gym or getting some mileage on my running shoes; I only regret the days I don't.

The same is true about spiritual workouts, especially when I read my Bible. It has been a process to read it. The more I seek God and "show up" by spending time in the Word, the more I exercise those spiritual muscles and build endurance. It doesn't matter if I read a verse, a paragraph, or a chapter; I am always grateful that I did. Some days, it is not easy to have that discipline. Other days, I get lost in the Word, and I become so grateful for all that God has done for my life. Instead of hanging up the phone with Jackie, we start a whole new conversation about reading our Bibles and the effects of them on our lives. Let us just say that we waited until our cellphone batteries were low to end the conversation.

We came to a couple of conclusions. Our first conclusion was we would love to drop off our bodies at the gym and have someone work it out for us and pick it up when all the taco calories are burned off, but the reality is that we must do the work. The second conclusion was that the same concept applies to our Bibles. I personally wish I had all the biblical knowledge and wisdom, but without opening my Bible, I am not going to get that depth and understanding that I desire.

The working out or "spiritual cardio" we do is necessary. Our trials and sufferings also act as our workouts that we must face to build that endurance. They are necessary to the process and to the building of the endurance that will help us grow and strengthen our walk with Jesus. The more endurance we build, the stronger we become against the lies and attacks of the enemy. Through that same endurance, there comes a joy from obedience. Most people claim to love God. The Word of God says in John 14:15 (NIV) that when you genuinely love God, you follow the commandments: "If you love me, keep my commands."

Anything that we value in our lives requires work, including relationships, school, health, and spiritual growth, to name a few. The work we dedicate to certain areas of our lives shows us what we think is important. What you dedicate your time to is a great indicator of what you value; therefore, where your treasure lies.

Let me share a few more cheesy exercise and sports references. As an athletic trainer, I have worked with a variety of athletes ranging from both endurance and strength sports. Let me tell you: the endurance sports ones usually are the ones that do not get the glory or the praise. It may have a lot to do with our culture and society. I mean, we dedicate almost a whole week to football. *Friday Night Lights*, Saturday *College Game Day*, and of course Sunday NFL. This is not even including *Monday Night Football* or *Thursday Night Football*.

Yes, there are running channels. I realize there is a market for everything. I am just saying people overlook the little guys. I personally love all sports. My career consists of watching sporting events. I would be in the wrong profession if I didn't like sports. My intentions are not to praise one sport over the other. There is intense hard work, discipline, and dedication to any sport. That said, let me tell you about runners. I have a love/hate relationship with this population. Not necessarily with the individuals, but with the process of the entire sport. This is coming from the healthcare professional; basically, I'm complaining, and I am not even the one running.

For the sake of arguments, I will focus on cross country only to make my point. Cross country is a year-round sport. There is no off-season, maybe a no-competing season, but they never stop running, ever. Yes, everyone who runs is a runner, but not everyone is an athlete. I think we can all learn from these athletes' disciplines and practices.

A runner is awake hours before even the sun hits the snooze button. While most of us are in our fifth dream, this person is lacing up their shoes, moving, warming up, and preparing for the miles they are about to put in. They have their warmup routine or ritual, they have a plan, and they get started. Contrary to popular belief, there are awfully specific training plans that have to be even more specialized and differentiated for each individual. They may have the same goal or race in the end, but they have their own skills, tools, and talents to develop.

A runner goes outside whether there is rain or shine. They know that any deviation from their plan may jeopardize their progress. When a runner has an injury, most resulting from overuse, they know exactly what is off with them. They can identify a moment or circumstance that led to the injury. They know that something is wrong and are actively taking measures to deal with, treat, heal, and prevent the problem from progressing. These measures may include a warm-up protocol, foam rolling, stretching, heat packs, cryotherapy, manual therapy, and anything else in the therapeutic world you can think of.

Serious runners can become annoyingly obsessive (I write this in love) about their injuries. It is an admirable trait when reasonable. As the one overseeing their health, I cater to the different needs of each athlete to heal them from the pain and stress placed on their bodies. Despite the pain, they keep pushing and keep moving forward. They have setbacks, of course, but when they are unable to do the miles on land, they re-adjust and resort to pool workouts or other low-impact alternatives. A runner usually hangs out with other runners; only they will understand why while everyone else is indulging in birthday cake and party food, this person is by the random veggie table avoiding the ranch dipping sauce with their water bottle.

Runner friends will give each other that eyebrow raise nod across the room, signaling that it is time to leave even though it's only 10 p.m. They have each other's backs because they know rest is needed for the ten-miler "recovery run" that Sunday morning. I know, we normal people think that is crazy, but that is their world. Those are the necessary disciplines that must be acted out for that individual to be successful in their field. People will go to spectate these racing events, which are exciting and inspirational. The amount of time and dedication that the individual invested makes us believe that we could do it too. God has yet to place that desire in my heart, so we are still speaking hypothetically. Here is my analogous interpretation between running and Christianity.

- Runners have a goal to win a race. Christians have a race with a goal to lead others to Christ and ultimately make it (and flourish) in heaven, as stated in Hebrews 12:1 (NIV): "Therefore, since we are surrounded by such a great cloud of witnesses, let us throw off everything that hinders and the sin that so easily entangles. And let us run with perseverance the race marked out for us."

- Runners prevent injuries by taking preventive measures such as warming up, stretching, and prehab. Christians prevent spiritual injury by starting the day putting on the full armor of God, and their prehab is prayer and reading the Word, as stated in Ephesians 6:11 (NIV): "Put on the full armor of God so that you can take stand against the devil's schemes."

- When there is injury, runners take necessary measures to treat those injuries. When sin occurs, Christians should take immediate action to resolve the problem. Confess, repent, and walk forward in faith and in the Word (Bible), preparing to prevent the next injury to our hearts and souls.

- Runners surround themselves with people that share the same goals and vision, thus encouraging each other to stay committed to their goals. Christians should surround themselves with other like-minded Christians that will encourage each other to continue with our walk and to walk in humble obedience, as stated in Ecclesiastes 4:12 (NIV): "Though one may be overpowered, two can defend themselves. A cord of three strands is not quickly broken."

- Runners follow a strict diet (lifestyle). Christians should follow a strict spiritual diet (lifestyle and walk) that feeds and nourishes our souls, such as reading the Word, praying, and fasting. What we feed ourselves is what we will be. We can feed our spirit or our flesh. The one that is stronger is the one you feed. There is a saying, "You are what you eat," and it is applicable and relatable. Reference Romans 8:6 (NIV): "The mind governed by the flesh is death, but the mind governed by the Spirit is life and peace."

There is a fitness quote that goes something along the lines of "You cannot outwork a bad diet." In fitness terms, this means that all the exercise that you do will not help you achieve your goals because there is still an unbalance of energy (calories). Calories in exceed the calories out, so despite "working out," you are still on the gaining weight spectrum. I said gaining weight because I am always in the "trying-to-lose-weight mode." If you are on the opposite of this conundrum, attempting to gain weight is just as difficult, if not more.

So yes, exercise is great for you, but if you are not eating the proper foods and nutrients needed to reach your goals, it is impossible to achieve that goal. For Christianity, we can attend all the services, listen to worship, do devotionals all we want, but we will never fully embrace all the benefits of a healthy, spiritual diet until we actually read our Bibles, pray, and fast and journal. At least, this was the case in my life.

I had been a churchgoer for as long as I can remember. It was just what we did. There was a general knowledge of the stories and, of course, the miracles that Jesus did, but my knowledge was still very superficial. Even now that I have read through the Bible and have made real efforts to study and understand it, I still feel like I am seeing it for the first time. I did not know what people meant when they said that the Bible was alive. I would roll my eyes and think they were just wanting to sound "extra." Now that I am slightly a little more mature, I get what they were talking about. Anyone can read the Bible logically, but when you pray and ask the Holy Spirit to illuminate the Word and speak to you, that is how we can understand the mind of God! It was never a book about God; it is a book of God speaking to us!

Let me share a random flashback. I have an older brother. When we were younger, my mom would always have everything blue for him and everything pink for me, even our sippy cups. My mom seriously wanted a girly-girl ballerina-type daughter (sorry, Mom! I love you!).

She took our gender roles so seriously that I was never allowed to drink chocolate Nesquik, just strawberry. If that is not a sin, then I do not know what is. Do not get me wrong: I have nothing against strawberry; in fact, I never complained about drinking it. I was okay with drinking strawberry milk for years until that one glorious day, my brother got up to go to the kitchen, and I went all Eve and had a sip of his cup. I tasted the sweetest of sweets, chocolate. Where had chocolate been my whole life? Okay, my whole life was about four years at this moment but still. It's like if my mom would have decided for me that I was to only like strawberry milk and never let chocolate be a contender. In the words of Cher from *Clueless*, "As if?" It took me discovering chocolate for myself, tasting the sweetest of sweets, that I knew there was no going back. Disclaimer: I do like strawberry, but it is not my go-to. Shout out to all the strawberry lovers.

The way I see this is that I can listen to sermons, podcasts, Christian radio, or anyone talking about the Word, and it is good, like strawberry (for me). But when I hear others talk about God and His word, it is like I am being told what they think about it, that I should like it because it came from them. Do not get me wrong. I love learning, and I grow so much because of others. In fact, reading and listening from others was how I started my walk. God anoints leaders and places leaders in their positions of spiritual authority so that we can learn from them. Much of my initial learning that happened in my life was from going to church and hearing the Word. It was still strawberry. But when I read my Bible, chocolate overflows. I don't only hear from others how good God is because I read it and know for myself. Reading the Word and hearing the same thing being preached increases my faith. It is all for spiritual growth.

We are never going to be perfect; that is a given. We don't have to earn God's love. That is what the cross means. We do, however, have to work at becoming more like Christ every day. That happens by reading the Word, meditating on it, and applying it to our own lives.

We (and by we, I mean, me too) do not want to read the Bible because it convicts us. Honestly, what is so bad about conviction? I get it. Trust me, I do. It is hard to look at the mirror and see our roots, our flaws, and the ways we are disappointing God. God already knows all the mistakes we have made; He knows the ones we will make too, and He still loves us more than anything. That is why we have convictions, not condemnation. Conviction leads to repentance; condemnation sends us straight downstairs. Reference Romans 8:1–2 (NIV): "Therefore, there is now no condemnation for those who are in Christ Jesus, because through Christ Jesus the law of the Spirit who gives life has set you free from the law of sin and death."

God wants us to come running back to Him and away from everything that pulls us from Him. Anything that pulls us from God is not God. God does not like it when we sin. He hates it, in fact. Every time we sin, it is a sin against God; it does not matter what the sin is. The spiritual practices are there for a reason, to strengthen our hearts and our faith. We should be like those endurance athletes and take care of our spiritual bodies with such passion by reading, meditating, and living the Word.

Crowning Moment

Picking up the Word of God, reading, and finding answers for myself.

Armor of God: Shoes (The Gospel of Peace)

That everywhere I walk, I can share His peace and the good news!

Verse to Remember

"Therefore, since we are surrounded by such a great cloud of witnesses, let us throw off everything that hinders and the sin that so easily entangles. And let us run with perseverance the race marked out for us" (Hebrews 12:1, NIV).

CHAPTER 11

Hummingbird

"My hummingbird" is what he would say to me as he embraced me in a larger-than-life hug. That was my favorite place to be. My spot, I would refer to the space on his shoulder where my head would lie. I belonged there. I thought he was the only man to see me and know me. When I describe the perfect man, he is it. The relationship that lasted the shortest was the one to have such a powerful impact on my life. This man was the best thing to ever happen to me; however, we got it all wrong. He saw me in the rawest form of myself and accepted me entirely as I was. I should have done the same for him. I did not and could not understand why it was so impossible for us to be together. We made sense; at least in my mind, we did. However, we were fighting an uphill battle before we even got started.

This man gave me hope. He was the man I dated after enduring an abusive relationship. I should not have put the weight of my pain on him. Not a lot of time had transpired between the end of the abusive relationship to the beginning of this one. This man had already come into my life, but he resurfaced when I needed him the most.

At the time this relationship developed, we were two broken individuals trying to mend each other's wounds without helping ourselves first. Pain brings people together; I now see it as the reason why we gravitated so heavily to each other. I recently learned the term "trauma bonding," and it made sense. Our feelings and our sufferings brought us together, and we wanted to be there for each other.

We were in such a vulnerable place. I loved that vulnerability, though; it was dark in a weird way. Was this what love was supposed to feel like? When I would spend time with him, the universe froze, and it was just the two of us. Nothing else mattered. I remember lying on the floor next to him, staring at the ceiling. He would serenade me with acoustic songs. Was this real life? It seemed like a dream, a foggy memory; confusion was the prevailing feeling of this relationship. Insert "Out of the Woods" by Taylor Swift.

I was never sure of what he felt. Did he know how much he meant to me? If only he could see himself through my eyes. How can someone this kind and loving exist, especially after all the pain that he endured? He was my comforter, and I was trying to be his. He was healing my heart, and I was working to heal his. He was my protector from my ex-boyfriend, and I had never felt so safe in the presence of any other man before. We should have been cautious because of the current conditions of our hearts. We didn't know any better. The more we tried to make the relationship work, the more that the obstacles and toxic people came trying to knock us down.

After the heartbreak that led me to God, I had made the decision to live for Christ. However, we don't change automatically when we make that decision. I was in the transitional stage from baby Christian to finding out what a Christian walk would look like in my life. God was holding my hand firm enough to keep me from going back to that previous relationship, but now, it was time for me to figure out if I was going to live for Him or revert to my same ways and behaviors before Christ. This man was everything that I wanted, but I wanted God more. I wanted him, but my heart and soul ached for God. I couldn't shake the conviction that following Jesus required saying goodbye to the past and letting go of things and people who did not align to God's Word and will. I wanted to be with this man, but I wanted to walk in obedience more.

It was a Thursday morning when I texted him that I wanted to talk to him. He asked me if everything was okay. I replied. "Yes, I am just thinking about some things that I want to talk to you about." We decided to meet for dinner at our favorite restaurant. It was his spot. He was a regular there, but it became my spot too, for a while. I arrived at the restaurant, and he was sitting on the restaurant bar looking down at his hands. He resembled a kid who had just been placed on time-out. My heart sank. I felt a knot in the throat, similar to when you watched *Titanic* for the first time, and you didn't want to cry. I didn't want to hurt him. I thought, *I do not want to hurt this man, not him, God.*

He looked up with such sadness in his eyes. He knew what was coming; he had been here before. I did not know how to begin. How could I tell him that I wanted to be with him but could not be with him because he was not a Christian enough without sounding like a complete jerk? I had literally spent the entire day trying to come up with the words to say to him. I even practiced on my bathroom mirror. It sounded sane and logical to me. *He will understand, and this will be an amicable breakup,* I thought.

Friends, the words that came out of my mouth were nowhere near sane, logical, or anything close to that realm. All it took was one look at those puppy eyes, and my mind was jello. My brain was useless. For the life of me, I could not remember one of the sentences that I had "mastered" just a few minutes earlier. If I could go back in time to prevent birthing this awkward conversation, I would. I uttered: "I do not think we should see each other anymore. The more I grow in my faith, the more I believe that I should be dating someone who shares the same faith as me. I just cannot see how this will work out."

Before I continue, I had told him about my relationship with God, and he was supportive. He had even agreed to go to church services with me. He was also okay with me wanting to honor God in my relationship, even though he did not agree or understand. However, I felt guilty about asking him to do or not do something that was not in his belief system.

"How long have we been dating, Andy?" he asked. "A little over a month," I replied. "So, you are telling me that you had a month to change me into the Christian man who you wanted, and because it did not happen now, you are going to dump me?" Ouch, that was painful to hear. He wasn't right, but he wasn't wrong all entirely. The conversation went on, and of course, I felt like a selfish person for the way I went about telling him my feelings. How does one explain being unequally yoked? I barely understood it at this point. How do you tell him that you want someone who shares the same faith as you so that if you were to stumble, the other would help keep the focus on Jesus and not on self?

Ending this relationship was heartbreaking. I kept thinking to myself that I had not even given it enough time to see if he would make those changes for the sake of us. I doubted myself and my judgment. I knew that it was the right decision by the peace that I felt letting go. I am sure we could have found a way to make it work, but that would have been ignoring what God was asking of me. I would have been ignoring the conviction that God gave me and been telling God that my way was better than His way. We have to trust God when He is closing the door. When I doubt what God is trying to tell me, I go back to these three questions that I got from Kait Warman in *The Heart of Dating* podcast that I believe she got from Lysa TerKeurst:

1. Is God good?
2. Is God good to me?
3. Do I trust God to really be God in all things?

Crowning Point

Learning that God is still good, even when certain decisions didn't make sense to me, especially when they were conflicting with my feelings.

Armor of Choice: Shield of Faith

Trusting that God has a better will for my life than me.

Verse to Remember

"The heart is deceitful above all things and beyond cure. Who can understand it?" (Jeremiah 17:9, NIV).

CHAPTER 12

Don't Poke the Sleeping Bear

All of us have been through some type of trauma in our lives and struggle with our unique insecurities. In this season of my life, my biggest struggle was dealing with singleness (don't roll your eyes; I know, first world problems). I can gladly say that I am currently loving and embracing my state of singleness because I am using this time to build myself, cultivate new friendships, and strengthen existing relationships.

I did not get to where I am today from one day to the next. It was a transitional period that required work. Transition is a skill that must be practiced. Before I got to this breakthrough in my faith, I had to go through yet another breakdown. (Again, because of my disobedience, I did not have to, but God allowed it for my shaping.)

Am I the only one that notices the pattern of how God is always trying to mold me? I can imagine Him being the potter, me the clay, and God saying, "Nope, this is not what I was molding you to be; do-over." Thank God, He is patient. The Word of God says in Isaiah 64:8 (ESV): "But now, O LORD, you are our Father; we are the clay, and you are our potter; we are all the work of your hand."

I had recently returned from a trip to New York City. When I travel, I try not to bring back too many souvenirs or trinkets. I learned my lesson because everything I buy for myself ends up in a storage box forever.

My brother and I were on a mission, though, to find and purchase a very specific New York taxicab magnet as per a request from our mother. This taxicab magnet sent us on a scavenger hunt all along Times Square. I gave up on the magnet and ended up getting the usual coaster and souvenir mug.

As I looked down into my purse and started to reach for my wallet, something caught my attention from the corner of my eye. I focused on it. *Yes*, I thought, *This is perfect. He is going to love it.* It was a back scratcher. It was adjustable and had the typical I Love NY logo written on it. He used to have one. I did not know if he still did. His was wooden, though, and it was old and chewed up in one corner. He would claim that the chewed-up part was the key to this said back scratcher being extra special. He would always have it within reach, especially after his knee surgery to scratch the itches that were too far.

Who is he, you might ask? See "Hummingbird" chapter. When I began writing about him, it was excruciating. I placed myself back in time and relived everything. I looked at the relationship from a new perspective and continued to understand why God meant for that relationship not to be successful. I felt that I was in a good place after reflecting. In those weeks that God put in my heart to journal about him, I was constantly thinking about him. I was trying to ask God why He wanted me to write about this man who was never mine; he was my almost. Ironically, the song "Almost Lover" from A Fine Frenzy was the song I grieved this almost-relationship to. It isn't a Christian song, but it is so beautiful and relatable to those "almosts" in our lives. I was thinking about him consistently, and this is why I believe that soul ties are real and so powerful.

I was sitting down poolside at my own birthday party, looking at the ripples in the water, thinking of ripple effects in my life—pretty deep thoughts for a birthday. I kept thinking how every choice that I had made had led me to be so immensely blessed to have my girlfriends throw a surprise *Office*-themed birthday party for me on this particular day.

In my thankful thinking, as I was watching the water, I saw his face in my mind. In less than a minute later, he sent me a video. My heart sank. I ran to the closest restroom. I washed my face and looked at myself in the mirror. I said to myself: *Chill, get it together. I know it is just a video, but why was he sending this to me now? I had not heard anything from or about him in about a year. Is this from You, God, or is it the enemy trying to destroy me? It was a surprise birthday party. My birthday was not for another week. He couldn't have been just texting me coincidentally to wish me a happy birthday.*

What I did next, I do not recommend for anyone who is in the process of healing and letting go. My situation taught me a lesson, but it could have been learned without the added pain. I opened a door that I had closed a long time ago. I knew it would be difficult, but I thought this was a door that was "safe" to open. I don't know if it came from God to open this door, and I do not know what would have happened if that door had stayed closed.

We don't like change because change is essentially trauma. Change can be for good or for the lesser. Change is the one thing that is constant, even though we may not want it. We want to stay in places longer: in relationships longer, in moments longer. We go through trials and struggles. We are always in the battle with forces, both seen and unseen. Those battles and changes are necessary for our faith and spiritual growth. As we mature little by little, we start to see and understand that there is a reason for the trials and a purpose to our pain. We recognize that what lies ahead is so much better than what we are clinging to. The words "the best is yet to come" become a daily encouragement sentence we write in lipstick on our bathroom mirror. We start to understand that what we cling to will determine our future. Do we cling to the old, or will we embrace what is new? Will we let go of old habits to accept new responsibilities?

Update: I met up with Hummingbird. Yes, we are calling him that from now on. I would be lying if I said that it wasn't so, so, so good to see him. I was working on this project specifically, and I was the one to reach out. I just missed him; I had no ulterior motives, pinky promise! Before he arrived at the café I was sitting at, I prayed: *God, please protect my heart. I do not know or understand why I am seeing him again. Please, do not let me feel pain. Show me what You want me to learn from this conversation. You know how nervous I am at this moment; calm me. Help me be still. If at any moment I begin to miss him or have feelings of going back, remind me of my why. You are my why. You will always matter more. Above all else, Lord, I love You.*

I recognized his walk before I even saw his face. I had a mini heart attack at the realization of the shirt that I was wearing. My shirt said, "All I want is Jesus and all the dogs." I wasn't ashamed of the shirt, but I thought to myself that it would probably be hurtful or even rude to him because our relationship had ended because of my decision to follow Jesus. I thought he might see it as an insult or a slap in the face. He saw me. I stopped breathing for a few seconds. His presence still gets me sometimes. His smile was so big, followed by an even bigger hug. Phew, I was in the clear. I do not know if he thought of anything of the shirt, but I was not going to dare ask. We sat down and talked.

It was a nice conversation; I saw that even though only one year had gone by, I was a different woman than I was back when he and I were an item. I had intentionally changed my heart. I had been focusing on my walk with Christ and had grown spiritually. I don't claim to know his heart and say that he hadn't changed in a year; we all do. Change is inevitable. I had a difficult year, and God was walking with me through it all. How did I do it before? I remembered how my life was before God. I was just wandering by. I was so lost before; even now, I keep stumbling.

I don't know how or why God chose and constantly chooses to fight for me when I do not deserve His love and mercy, but I am so glad that He did. I know that I will stumble and fall, but I am falling forward. When I fall hard on my face, all I have to do is look up and reach for the hand that is laid out before me. He never lets go; it has always been me. This time around, though, His grip on the palm of my hand is firm because it is not just Him holding on. I am holding on, too. Even though I stubbornly look back and think that I miss my old life, I know that what lies ahead with God is far better than any plan that I could have made for myself.

Crowning Moment

I cannot go back to the past. Some doors are meant to stay closed. Remind myself of the decision I made to stay strong in temptation. God is still molding me.

Armor of Choice: Shield of Faith

My faith has to be greater so that I am not swayed by my emotions that are very real.

Verse to Remember

"But now, O LORD, you are our Father; we are the clay, and you are our potter; we are all the work of your hand" (Isaiah 64:8, ESV).

CHAPTER 13

May the Fourth

He (my next, next, next relationship, okay, this is
getting embarrassing) and I had already made the decision to get married. Only two of my girlfriends knew.
On that day, we were headed to the beach for a running
event. The event was called Jailbreak, which is a 5K race
with obstacles on the beach. I was the one to organize
my group's participation in the event. He was the only
man present among seven of my girlfriends.

Here I was wearing a matching Dunder Mifflin T-
shirt with him and doing annoying couple things. I
could share this experience with him and with all my
girlfriends. He was quick to take on the role of the cour-
teous gentleman catering to all of us. There was no way
I was jealous; my girlfriends kept telling me how lucky
I was, and I really was. I was so in love with him. I was
finally with a man that prioritized me and loved me so
well. There were red flags along most of our relationship, but as they say, love is blind. After the race, we
set up a canopy and sat down on our pink and green

his-and-hers beach chairs; mine was green, obviously. There was a group of people camped out in front of us. One of the men in that group kept looking in our direction. I mean, it was obvious why. We were a group of beautiful young women...and my fiancé.

He and I were frequent gym-goers. I was always trying to lose weight; he was always trying to get bigger. The strange man who was obviously after my friends was physically fit. My boyfriend kept looking at me and telling me to stop looking at him. He kept asking if I wanted him to be that "big." My defenses automatically went up because there was no way that I was looking at this man in any other way other than him just being there.

I couldn't believe that he was jealous, even though he said it playfully. It was still jealousy. In my head, there was no one other than him; I didn't see any other men. I would daydream about him all the time, look at my screensaver, which was a picture of him, and give him every free minute of my life. I was consumed by him. My thoughts were as follows: *Why would he think that I was staring at another man? Did he really not believe how much I loved him? Did we not just decide to get married? Maybe I was looking at that guy?* Those thoughts plagued my head, and instead of noticing that those were his insecurities, I fell for the trap. I apologized for him being hurt. I reassured him that I was not looking at any other man than him. I stayed glued to him for the rest of the time we spent at the beach.

That same afternoon, we drove back earlier than the rest of the group. We had a birthday party for the baby of one of his friends to attend. We were exhausted but still agreed to go back to his friend's house after the actual party. His friends and their wives were all there. One of the friends, in particular, was visiting from out of town. He was the other single one in the group.

That whole group was into biking, so naturally, the conversation gravitated to, "My bike is better than yours." My fiancé decided to take his friend's bike for a quick spin. The friend from out of town started a conversation with me. I already knew the others, so I thought to myself, *Okay, this guy is trying to figure me out; see if I'm cool enough for his friend.* When my fiancé came back, his demeanor changed drastically. He really went from Happy to Grumpy; yes, I just used a Snow White reference. I didn't think much of it at first.

We left. I hopped into his truck, and as soon as I closed the door, he said, "So, do you want to sleep with him or what?" I couldn't believe that those words came out of his mouth. I thought I was imagining things; he had never said something so disrespectful to me. "Excuse me?" I replied. He then repeated the same question. We were on the back roads heading back to his house. I tried so hard not to be so sensitive. I was choking back the tears when I was finally able to mumble the words, "Take me home." Then, the floodgates opened.

Not only was I uncontrollably crying, I made him pull the truck over because I felt that I was going to throw up. That comment triggered a physical response because of the previous emotionally abusive relationship (the "Heartbreak" chapter). I later discovered that even if we forgive and move on, the trauma happened, and our bodies remember.

He saw how much his comment affected me. He was quick to apologize. He had to give me a few minutes to calm down. I could not stop crying. I was never a crier; why was I reacting this way? I was hugging my knees, and my head was in-between them rocking back and forth while the crying continued. The more I cried, the more shame I felt. I did not want him to think of me as that girl that cries every time her boyfriend says something mean just to get her way. I just physically could not stop.

"I can't do this," I said to him after I successfully wiped my tears and boogers off my face. I attempted to talk again, which was an epic failure, as the tears came back again. Seriously, people, it was fire hydrant style. I cringe thinking back at this moment, but oh, the pain was so real. It had nothing to do with him—okay, well, the comment yes.

I didn't realize at the time that I was still holding on to traumas from my previous relationship. Those traumas were the reason that I was reacting the way I was with him. Not only was I embarrassed for my reaction, but I was also made aware of just how broken I still was. I was just slapped with a truth bomb. There was no way to avoid it any longer. I knew that I had work to do. I wanted my marriage to be successful. I needed to address my unresolved issues and traumas so that I could be the wife that he needed me to be.

He and I talked about our feelings and about the steps that we were going to take to make our relationship and future marriage work. The next morning, we turned our marriage application into our church. It felt so right, so effortless. It was not a sporadic decision that we had made because we had gooey feelings for each other; we were making a commitment. We knew that we would have arguments and disappointment, but we had just overcome a trial in our relationship, and I was convinced that this love was the love that God had for me, forever.

I started to bring to light what I had kept in darkness, like Luke 8:17 (NIV) states: "For there is nothing hidden that will not be disclosed, and nothing concealed that will not be known or brought out into the open."

As I started to reflect on what I had kept hidden, I began to realize that I had been a victim of gaslighting, which is defined as "a form of psychological manipulation in which a person seeks to sow seeds of doubt in a targeted individual or in members of a targeted group, making them question their own memory, perception, and sanity." Even though my current boyfriend/ fiancé had not used this tactic of manipulation on me, I couldn't help but react toward him.

My ex would constantly "gaslight" me into thinking that everything I thought, said, or did was wrong and disrespectful. Words spoken over us over a period have tremendous power. With time, I started to believe the lies. He was rewiring the way my brain worked. I believed that I was thinking the thoughts my ex claimed I was thinking. I was past the walking-on-eggshells phase; I was full-on walking barefoot on shattered glass in the dark with no sense of direction, figuratively of course, but so very real inside my head. I thought my fiancé was the man that God sent to save me from my past, my hurts, and my traumas. That wasn't the case, though. There is only one who can save me, forgive me, and redeem me. His name is Jesus. I just did not know how to surrender and let Him heal me. I had been trying to keep it together and be strong, but those traumas happened and needed to be addressed.

We need to bring those lies that are not from God out of the darkness and shine light into them. The enemy wants to keep us isolated, afraid, ashamed, and hopeless. He doesn't want us to tell God about it—much less anyone else.

Friends, I would be lying if I told you that I am over it, even now. The truth is, healing for all of us does not happen overnight. I was ashamed that I went through something like this. I didn't fit the stereotype of the "abused woman." I felt that I was dumb and pathetic for allowing myself to even have been in an abusive relationship. After all, I thought, those women were there because they chose to be in those situations. They could have left if they really wanted to. I didn't want to be associated with those "types" of women. I was just terrified of what people would say or think of me. I thought that if I buried my past, my relationship with him deep in the back of my mind, it would be as if it never happened. The reality of the matter is that I was one of those women.

The more I bring my past hurts to light, the more I heal. I will repeat this and stress the importance of community. I know God put my girlfriends in my life to act as a fountain of healing that would never stop pouring love and grace. Trust me when I say that they have heard my story infinite times, yet every time I say it to them, they listen as if it were the first time. I never felt rushed or pressured to "get over it" by them. They could have so easily been like, "We have heard this story a million times. We have offered you our advice on the matter, and you keep making the same mistakes over and over again. We can't help you. We don't want to hear it anymore." That never once happened.

Throughout the process of grieving and self-healing, I began to understand Jesus in a whole new different way. As I drew closer to God's Word, I felt compassion for my trials and struggles from God alone. I understood. God knew the pain I was feeling; He felt it too. One Monday morning, I was in the middle of 6 a.m. treatments when I felt my phone vibrate in my back pocket. This was odd to me because no one texts me that early. When I am at work that early, all of my friends are still dreaming. The text was from Priscilla, which said, "Have you heard the song 'Scars' from I AM THEY?" I answered, "Yes," to which she responded, "I am thankful for your heartbreaks because He brought you here."

It was a simple text. To anyone else, it may have seemed insignificant even. God knew the battles I was facing that morning, and that "simple" text was a reminder of my why. Why God allowed, not caused, me to go through the heartbreak and pain: it led me back to *Him*. There are scars, and I am thankful for them.

Crowning Moment

I acknowledged that there was unresolved trauma in my life, and I began to work toward bringing the truth to light so that God could heal me.

Armor of Choice: Sword of the Spirit
(the Word of God)

It is a double-edged sword that cuts but heals. The truth about ourselves hurts, but that means that we're on the right path to healing.

Verse to Remember

"For there is nothing hidden that will not be disclosed, and nothing concealed that will not be known or brought out into the open" (Luke 8:17, NIV).

CHAPTER 14

Not All Christians Are Created Equal

I want to be completely honest with you because I know that we all struggle with temptations. It was in the middle of watching a testimony during a conference. At that moment, I had a vision. It was more like a suppressed memory that I was not even sure had occurred.

In my vision or suppressed memory, my ex-fiancé at the time of this memory and I had gone out of town for a friend's wedding. He and I were trying to have a God-honoring and God-glorifying relationship. To anyone from my past or people not in the Christian community, this seemed crazy. I would hear demeaning comments like, "You are waiting to have sex? It's not going to last like that. All men are the same, and they all want sex. You are never going to find a man that will wait. He is going to cheat on you."

Ladies, I know that godly men exist, and this man was respectful of my desires to be obedient to God. That was not enough, though. The Bible warns us about being together with unbelievers or being unequally yoked.

After my relationship that led to the heartbreak that pointed me to Christ, I would pray to God to send me someone who would go to church with me. My ex-boyfriend (the heartbreak that led to me to Jesus) would not even step inside church with me after the one time he went with me. He said that he knew a few of the people that he saw at church were horrible people. He would proceed to tell me how those men would always cheat on their wives and basically talk down on them.

Although those comments would break my heart, I would still quote Jesus and say, "It's not the healthy who need a doctor." Church is for the sick; we are all sick and in need of a Savior. I learned that dating an unbeliever is never a good idea; at least in my case, it proved to be true. It says it in the Bible. The other thing I learned was to be extremely specific when you pray.

The following is what my prayers would sound like then (just remembering them now makes me laugh at myself): "Lord, please send me a man who is good. Send me a man who will go to church with me and will worship You with me. God, You know me better than I know myself, so please send me someone I will be attracted to both spiritually and physically (yes, we have established my vainness). I thank You for everything that You are doing in my life and trust in You, Lord. I ask this in Jesus' name. Amen."

When I met my fiancé, I knew he was an answered prayer. He was tall, handsome, and loved God. I remember going on that first date with him and thinking, *Wow, God. This is it. You did it in the blink of an eye.* I was so excited to get to know him. We just clicked; it was easy and exciting. Ironically, I met him, and a few days later, I had to leave for Costa Rica on yet another work trip. I remember this time not wanting to go because I had just met this man.

I was on the mountains, looking at the sky, and remembering how broken I had been just a year ago. Now, I had joy because of the hope and promise of this new man in my life. I anxiously waited for any Wi-Fi locations so that I could talk to him. I thought, *Wow, God. Thank You for Costa Rica. What is it about this place that every year I have been here, I have been in a completely different situation?* Here is a brief recap of my Costa Rica visits:

1. Soccer work trip. I was still with my ex-boyfriend (Tulum chapter), and he was happy that I was gone so that I could give him space. No relationship with God at this point. Just Sundays.

2. Soccer work trip. I was heartbroken because of the heartbreak that led me to Christ, which would eventually lead me to seek God.

3. Mission trip. The heartbreak was still in my life, trying to get back together with me. I had met Jesus. God had begun the healing process in my life. I was seeking Him more, attending church twice a week, finding godly friendships who would encourage me in my walk, and had started reading my Bible (Bible app devotionals)—I had to start somewhere.

4. Soccer work trip. I had met the fiancé. I thought this was the man God had for me. God did give me a great man who was a believer and went to church to worship with me.

At that point, that was enough for me because the previous relationships did not want anything to do with God. It was okay that we had not fully "gotten it" because we were both actively seeking and growing.

I learned the hard way that not all Christians are created equal, and there is a difference between being a believer and a follower of Christ (this applies to me, too). A believer knows that God exists, attends church, and may pray occasionally. This person says, "I am going to church. I am a good person. I do not give the full ten percent because that is a bit extreme, but I will slip a twenty every once in a while when the ushers pass. I do not cause anyone any harm and do not do evil." This person is the person checking the boxes, thinking, *I went to church: check.*

A follower of Christ loves God above all else and walks with Christ in obedience, in search of fulfillment of the purpose that God created them for. This person is working toward living a life in Christ, for Christ.

I do not mean to say that if you are in a relationship with a non-believer, it won't be successful. It may just be much more difficult because the people you surround yourself with influence you; it could be you influencing the non-believer to seek a relationship with Christ or the opposite, which is what happened to me.

In my relationship, we both started with God as our foundation, and it was great. I had never been in a mature relationship when we would pray first and then respond to our problems with biblical solutions. Dating a Christian does not exempt us from the messiness of relationships, but a person who fears the Lord is going to think about how they act toward you even when they are upset. When these situations occurred, we would try to solve the problem and get to the root of the issue and check ourselves if we were right to be upset.

If I did or said something that he felt was disrespectful or rude, he would approach me with honesty, and we would find a solution to the problem. It was the same way with him when he would show feelings of jealousy that were not because of me but because of previous traumas from prior relationships. We were so good at problem-solving and loving each other according to our love languages until we weren't.

He subtly started to pull away. He stopped reading the Bible with me, altogether claiming he was busy. He stopped doing devotionals on the Bible app, both with me and on his own. He stopped sending me verses and praying with or for me. He stopped talking about how God was working in his life. He stopped being thankful and started becoming entitled and resentful. He stopped attending weekday services because he was too tired. I understood; I was tired, too.

We traded doing healthy activities like biking for spending time with our other friends doing non-churchy things. It became easier for me to stop doing certain spiritual disciplines, even when I may have had the most spiritual day the day before, aware of what God was doing in my life, and could feel the goosebumps of the Holy Spirit.

Each day is a new day, a new creation, and a blank slate. We must surrender each day separately to God. Just like any other day, when we dress ourselves and prepare for the day ahead, we have to clothe ourselves with the full armor of God to be able to walk in God's will, be wise and strong enough to resist the attacks of the enemy. I wish I had known this sooner.

As I saw him become idle to certain spiritual practices, I also wanted to do less churchy things and spend more time with the man I loved. I knew he loved me, but I wanted him to desire me. I became flirtier in the way that I would talk and act around him. I loved the attention that he was giving me because I felt that validation that he was attracted to me and wanted to be with me. I skipped church that week prior to my friends' wedding for no reason other than to wait at home for him to get out of work.

I knew what I was doing, but it was like I was watching myself and not being able to stop. I knew the truth, yet I kept acting in disobedience to God. We have free will and the liberty to make our choice. Even then, God always gives us a way out. Something was changing in me, though: before, when I would sin, I didn't really care; I would "fake repent" and do it all over again. Something had changed now. This time around, when I fell into sexual sin, my heart broke. I couldn't fully understand it; I thought I would be okay with still doing things my way and asking for forgiveness. Not this time, though. I now was beginning to understand that my life wasn't my own. God had paid the price for me; He rescued me. What was this pain I was feeling? It physically hurt my heart. It wasn't my heart that was hurting; it was God's. I had intentionally hurt Him, the one who has always loved me. I was the one that kept pushing our boundaries, and before we knew it, we had fallen. I was so ashamed I couldn't stop the tears. I knew that my fiancé was upset. I felt that he was upset because I was upset, not because of the sin itself. I was upset because it was my fault. I was the one who let myself be influenced by the world instead of the Word (Jesus).

We prayed, asked God for forgiveness, and promised that it wouldn't happen again. The thing was that we were relying on our own strength and not God's. I still kept moving the boundary line. In a way, I kept testing myself and God; take a guess as to who lost in this tug of war. More and more things became okay. Certain actions and behaviors suddenly did not seem as big a deal as before. Maybe I was being too "Christian." I mean, after all, God had brought this man and myself together, so why would not He bless the relationship?

If we sinned a couple of times, I was sure God would forgive us. That became my way of thinking. I continued to pull away just like he did. I was tired of being the only one putting effort into walking in God's way. It was much more attractive to do the opposite of God's way.

On a Friday morning, he and I headed to Laredo for the wedding. We arrived at the hotel and started getting ready for our friend's wedding. Back home, we had rules and boundaries (the ones I embarrassingly kept pushing). We kept telling each other that we were strong and that nothing was going to happen.

After I finished putting on my second earring, I proceeded to continue with my makeup. I do not know if there are any girl rules about what goes first: makeup or jewelry. I was starting on my liquid eyeliner—women will understand the intensity of this moment. He was sitting on the couch; I could see him looking at me through the reflection in the mirror. He stood up and walked toward me. He whispered in my ear just how beautiful I was. Of course, that is something any woman loves to hear from her fiancé. In that moment, I thought I was lucky to be loved this way.

I'll spare you the details of what happened next. The shame was even heavier on my heart. I didn't know what to do with myself. I had made the choice again to sin. I couldn't understand.

Just a few weeks prior, I shared my testimony with a few of my girlfriends, and both he and I felt that we were so far away from immoral sin. We were strong and confident. That was when we were seeking God. This time, I couldn't physically look at him. I was so upset, sad, and ashamed. I was upset at myself because I had let myself get to that point. I knew what I had stopped doing.

I knew I wasn't strong in my relationship with my Father. I was weak. I could see myself pulling away and did not do anything to stop myself. I wouldn't talk to my girlfriends as much because I wanted to spend as much time as I could with him. When my girlfriends would ask me how I was doing, I would talk about how perfect my life was and about how good God was. They were happy for me, of course, and they did not notice that I had slowly started to isolate myself from them. I isolated myself from the people who were always there to lead me back to the cross, to my Father. They just understood that I wanted to spend more time with him.

My fiancé used to be my accountability person. If we saw ourselves start to stray, we would redirect each other to the truth. This time, I was angry at him. I started to blame him. I needed him to be strong for me because I was weak sometimes. It was not fair. I would tell him. I look back and remember me scolding him like a child. He was ashamed and sad that he could barely keep eye contact with me. I was mad at myself and at him.

This all happened before my friend's wedding, and it made my stomach churn to walk into a church. How was I supposed to go into a church knowing what I had just done? (*This is a lie from the devil himself. He wants us to feel ashamed, sinful, unworthy to keep us from the church, whether that be a physical building or the body of Christ in general, a lie that I was listening to, which is why I was subtly isolating myself from my girlfriends.*) We had a serious conversation about what had just occurred. I kept stressing the importance of both of us being strong and told him, "If you are going to be the man I marry, I need you to be there to pick me up when I fall, encourage me, and lead me back to God."

Instead of both of us praying and asking for forgiveness, I made him pray for us. I could not look at him still. I was fuming and bitter. It was wrong for me to blame him. I know it was very immature of me, but I was upset and wanted him to feel the conviction too. I kept thinking: *You pray. You made me fall. You led me to sin. Why am I the only one falling apart over here?*

This, of course, was not me acting out of love. It was resentment because of the hurt I was feeling. When he started praying for our relationship with each other and with God, he froze. It was as if he had forgotten how to pray altogether. I don't mean that when we pray, we have to use churchy words like "thous" and "O Great Merciful Father." I mean simply talking to God. It didn't click to me until recently that maybe the reason that he could not pray was that he had not been praying, probably for a long time.

It is easy to make yourself look like a Christian: you attend services, send scripture to your group chats, and say "God bless you" when someone sneezes. I can play the part too. Most people would not even have given it a second thought. I know why I chose to ignore the red flags. I was emotionally invested and wanted to be with him. I think both men and women fear being alone at some point in our lives. I kept thinking, *Well, I mean, we are going to get married, so maybe the sin is not that bad.* Sin is sin, though; it doesn't matter how you sugarcoat it.

That same night, I stopped breathing. I woke up in the middle of the night, and I was unable to breathe or move. I began to panic. Out of the corner of my eye, I could see him side-lying, giving his back to me. I was terrified and started to feel that there was someone, something, or a darkness in the room with us. I could feel the tears roll down my cheeks. I do not know how much time passed, but it seemed like time was still.

I began to pray. Just moments after praying for God to help me, I gasped and finally was able to breathe and break free. I started crying because I was still afraid of what had just happened. I looked over at him. He was snoring, unbothered. I felt even more resentful thinking, *I almost died, and you're just there snoring!* I felt sad all over again. I asked myself, *Is God trying to tell me something? Is this not the man for me?* More sadness overcame me. At this point, it was past 3 a.m., and I was exhausted. I thought to myself, *I am too tired for this. I will think about it in the morning.* I was leaving for Israel the next morning, and we still had a three-hour drive, and I had to pack. Procrastinating is my thing.

I went to Israel and did not think about that night again. I went to Israel and selfishly prayed for this marriage to work. I prayed for God to bless it, even though I already knew in my heart that it wasn't right. I was going to marry him. We had made plans. I had already secured the dress, the bridesmaids, and venue. I couldn't be at peace, though. Even though I wanted this relationship to work with all my strength, God knew that it wasn't the right relationship.

One day after my trip, we were sitting in my living room and ended it. The lack of peace I had up until the moment was so tangible that I knew it had to be done. I was heartbroken again, but I felt peace. I began to mourn and rejoice in what God had done. I thought, *God, if he wasn't the one, why did You bring him into my life?!*

I did learn that God blessed me with this man, showing me that when the time and my heart were right, He could do it in the blink of an eye. He answered my prayer. It is like a father when you beg him to let you eat all the junk food for breakfast, lunch, and dinner. He allowed it to happen to show me even though that was what I wanted, it was not healthy or sustainable. It literally gave me stomach pains!

It wasn't until I heard the testimony of a young man in a conference. The Wednesday before I went to that conference, our pastor had been talking about how many people are blinded, not completely, meaning that they are walking around with a spiritual veil over their eyes. The testimony I heard was so powerful in my life: it was about some of the ways that God gets our attention, and it isn't always pretty. I felt as if the veil was torn off before my eyes. I started to see what I couldn't see just one month ago before the breakup—what I did not want to see and accept. I wanted to slap myself. I felt so dumb.

I later found myself on WebMd's webpage and self-diagnosed myself. The scientific explanation of what happened to me was termed "sleep paralysis," which means the following: *feeling of being conscious but unable to move. It occurs when a person passes through the stages of wakefulness and sleep. During these transitions, you may be unable to move or speak for a few seconds up to a few minutes. Some people may feel pressure or a sense of choking.*

Some of the information that I read also tied sleep paralysis to a supernatural experience because people who experienced sleep paralysis claimed to have felt other presences followed by fear. While most of these testimonials may be subjected to the mental, emotional, and spiritual health of the individual, I know in my heart that mine was spiritual. At first, I thought it was from the enemy because I had been afraid, and it was really dark. Through prayer, God gave me the revelation that it was a warning from Him. He was trying to show me what my life would be like if I stayed in that relationship: dark, full of fear, and no spiritual support. I did not know it was God at the time.

Crowning Moment

God cares more about protecting me than my feelings; He knows that I will be okay eventually. Like a father, He does not have to explain the reason for everything. I can trust that He has my best interest in mind. *I still trust.*

Armor I Needed: Sword of the Spirit

I needed the truth; I was not wanting to hear it, but the truth (Word of God) set me free.

Verse to Remember

"So, if you think that you are standing firm, be careful that you don't fall" (1 Corinthians 10:12, NIV).

CHAPTER 15

Blindsided

I thought the breaking up would be the hardest. It turns out that it was the easiest part of the process. I had the conviction and had been mourning it before we ended the relationship. I have heard it said, "If the battle is too big for you, it is not yours; it belongs to God." I knew what God had placed in my heart, and I knew that this battle was too big for me. Why do I try to control the outcome? Why do I try to tell God what to do? (As if I was smarter than the Creator of the entire universe.)

This is one of my bad habits. I believed that I knew what was best for me, and God was probably laughing at how microscopic my dreams were. It is expected to feel pain after a breakup. Why would I be an exception to the rule? My reasons for choosing to end the relationship were good, honest, and valid. By this chapter of my life, I had learned that if God tells me to do something, I do it—well, most of the time.

After breaking up my engagement, I felt empowered and right in my decision. I was being obedient to what

God wanted from me. I should have been happy, right? I learned that sometimes doing the right thing will hurt and that it is okay to be sad after making the right decision. There was great sadness in my heart. I prayed for God to heal me, and I wanted Him to do it immediately.

Now, let us discuss a slight detour (I have a point; I promise!). I would consider myself as someone with a high pain tolerance. Mind over matter, right? I have had all the bumps, bruises, scrapes, sprains, and strains. If I did not think about the pain, I would not feel it. Everything that I have read talks about the good in the pain. Pain is an indicator that something is wrong. There is a purpose for the pain. As C. S. Lewis said, "God whispers to us in our pleasures, speaks to us in our conscience but shouts in our pain."

The thing is sometimes, when you have been through seasons of pain after pain, you can become numb to it. At least, I did. That numbness came from the hardening of my heart. I thought I was guarding my heart, but it was really me laying down bricks that would eventually turn into a brick wall that would be impenetrable to any feelings, whether good or bad. That wall became so high, and I was safe. I was in my safe place, and I knew that because I controlled what was allowed inside, I would be in control of any possible pain in the foreseeable future. I avoided any situation or confrontation that I knew would bring me some form of discomfort.

As an avid knee scraper, control to me was like picking at a scab and opening the wound all over again, thus further delaying the healing process. No, it would not hurt like the initial pain or trauma, but it became addictive: reopening that scab, letting it heal a little, just to repeat the process a few more times. It was okay because I controlled the outcome.

When this breakup occurred, I would think to myself if I stayed busy and did not think about him, I would eventually be okay. If I could anticipate the pain that was coming, I could mentally prepare. I am not one to predict the future, so when unexpected storms occurred, I was caught unprepared in the middle of the storm without any help or supplies.

For those of you that have seen the show *Friends*, I was the spitting image of Ross from *Friends* with the margaritas claiming, "I'm fine." My reality of this emotional situation was that I was wet, shivering cold, and without so much as a flashlight for this storm of life. It was a self-inflicted storm, nonetheless, a storm. You would think that someone who was so controlling would be more prepared when these situations arose...Ironic.

I always thought that I was all alone in the dark, but I wasn't; I never have been. I had Word of God lighting my way out of the darkness, as Psalm 119:105 (NIV) states: "Your word is a lamp for my feet, a light on my path."

I may not know what my future will look like tomorrow, the next day, or even years from now. I do know, however, that God was with me in the storm. God was giving me just enough to make it out of that dark, cold place; figuratively, I live in South Texas, where it does not even get cold at Christmas. I just needed to listen to Him and take the first step, then the next right step, and so on. I know that when I feel lost, anxious, lonely, and hurt, I always have His Word to rescue me and help me out of the darkness.

I had been okay with the pain because that is how life is. Everyone goes through pain. What makes me think that I am immune to pain? If I expected it, I could control it. I was in control; I ended the relationship with this man because it was not aligning with God's will. I controlled when we would communicate post-breakup. I controlled the date and time that we would meet to exchange each other's belongings.

The unexpected occurred when he was outside my house waiting for me to come back from dinner with a girlfriend. I had just gotten done talking with my friend about the relationship and had the affirmation from her as well that I was doing the right thing. I repeat: doing the right thing does not void us of the feelings. Doing what is easy and what is right is not always aligned. Emotions can be so strong sometimes that sadness causes physical pain. Before I got off my car, I said the quickest prayer: "God, help. Amen."

His boots hit the pavement as he exited his lifted white Dodge Ram. The same truck that brought me excitement nerves the first time he picked me up for our first date was now giving me a feeling of being gut-punched on my stomach. He rolled my bike toward me and handed it to me. I shot him an awkward smile, attempting to avoid eye contact, and thought in my head, *God, if he is not the one for me, why did You make him so pretty?* He would hate that I am calling him pretty because he would argue that he is handsome.

He handed me a handful of books (our quality time was biking and reading together—not at the same time, we were not that talented). I thought, *I'm okay, I'm okay.* He handed me the folder that I asked him to bring me. The folder contained all the wedding details. There were still some vendors that we had to cancel, and the rest were under my name. It was my turn to grow up and make those calls. I grabbed the folder, which should have crushed me because it had all the plans for the wedding of my dreams with the person who I thought was the man of my dreams. That future that would be no longer.

He left. I did not look back. I closed the door behind me, bent down, and told Bailey (my beautiful pitbull mix), "We're going to be okay, Bailey." I nearly suffocated my poor baby to death from how hard I hugged her. The tears started coming down as if the flood gates to my soul had been opened. I started feeling extremely sick and made it to the restroom just in time to not have my dinner all over the restroom floor. Sorry, I know I write this often; I said I wanted to be real with you. I washed my face, and my cell phone vibrated. It was him. "Hey, is it okay if we go back? She wants to say goodbye to you."

This, my friends, was the unexpected. His daughter, who I had grown to cherish and love so much, was with him in the truck. I had not planned or expected to say goodbye to her: the little girl who would have become my stepdaughter, the one who would walk over to him and hand him the rings in our ceremony, and the one who would team up with me and bully her dad into watching girly movies with us because girls rule, boys drool.

How do I break up with her too? I loved her. I loved both so much, and I still had to say goodbye. I did not want her to feel rejection like I had in the past. My heart broke, thinking that this would have a negative impact on her life. I want her to feel loved, worthy, and know that she is enough. She deserved the whole world, and I was not going to be in her life anymore to play a part in it. I prayed: *God, if this is Your will, give me strength!*

In less than a couple of minutes, they returned. I do not know how I was able to keep my composure. She ran out of the truck and gave me a hug; you know, those types of hugs that you never want to break because you feel the love. I gave her a crooked smile—mainly because I was trying not to say much because she would notice the breaking of my voice. I proceeded to tell her that I was going to miss her and that I would always pray for her.

She started back to the truck, looked back, and waved goodbye. I waved back at her and tried not to look at him. I could not do that to myself again. I knew I had to follow through with the decision that I had made. It hurt, and by hurt, I mean everywhere. I was in shock at how much power our emotions have over our bodies. A simple text message from him made me nauseated. The thought of seeing him loosened everything in my stomach. I did not know heart pain was actual pain in my heart. The rest of that day, I cried until there were no more tears. I healed a little that day.

It takes work. I wish we could go from heartache to completely whole and healed in an instant, but there is a purpose to the process. I wish I could tell you why we go through what we go through. I do know that we grow through what we go through, if that can give you any comfort. For me, there was pain because I chose my will over God's, and I was not supposed to be in that relationship, even if it was an okay one. I wish I had the answers and all the healing for everyone. I do not have the answers, though. Only Jesus does. When I was going through this, I kept seeing this verse, James 1:2–4 (NIV): "Consider it pure joy, my brothers and sisters whenever you face trials of many kinds, because you know that the testing of your faith produces perseverance. Let perseverance finish its work so that you may be mature and complete, not lacking anything."

We live in a broken world. There is a lot of evil out there. There is a lot of pain. Because of sin, we deviated from God's perfect plan for our lives. Most of us will probably spend our entire lives trying to become the person that was in the original design. I can guarantee you that most of us will fail. I say this not to sound discouraging but to let you know: I will, too. I, too, feel pain, fall, and fail. I am ashamed, say, and do things that I wish I would take back. We should still try to become that person that God intended. Through faith and perseverance, we become like that person a little more each day.

Crowning Moment

Learning that doing the right thing will not void me of the feelings. It is okay to feel to heal.

Armor of Choice: Shield of Faith

Faith to trust God. Even though this was the breakup with my fiancé, it hurt less than with Hummingbird because my faith had increased, and He had shown me to be trustworthy.

Verse to Remember

"Trust in the Lord with all your heart, and do not lean on your own understanding. In all your ways acknowledge him, and he will make straight your paths" (Proverbs 3:5–6, ESV).

CHAPTER 16

New Moon

It was a Saturday night after what felt like a hundred-hour work week. I was watching the *Twilight* movie, *New Moon*. If that is not a singleness goal, then I don't know what is. Please, no judgment here. After all, I still remember going to the midnight premiere the day before I had my TAKS standardized benchmark back in high school. It was worth the sleepless night. I don't know why this is my favorite movie of them all. I know the storylines are probably better in the other books and movies, but this one was the most relatable to me. Even now, I find myself rewatching this movie when I have only seen the others a couple of times.

In *New Moon*, Bella is going through the seasons, literally: winter, fall, spring, and summer. She is writing emails to Edward and Alice. She receives no response from them. She says that she can almost forget that they existed because they have been gone for so long, but the pain that she feels is her reminder that they were real.

It made me wonder; how many times have I held on to pain because I wanted to feel that what I lost was real?

Yesterday, I heard a podcast regarding soul ties. Guys, I have like a million soul ties! I had no idea. Soul ties are not my area of expertise, but here is my understanding of them. Soul ties are defined as "emotional bonds that form an attachment. They may be godly or ungodly, pure, or demonic. Soul tie is a linkage in the soul realm between two people. It links their souls together, which can bring forth both beneficial results or negative results. Soul ties can be formed biologically, physically, emotionally, spiritually, and mentally. Some of these connections are destructive and ungodly."

Boy, oh boy! Is it any wonder I am such a mess? I don't know about you, but sometimes I feel less than whole. I know that through Christ, I am worthy, loved, and whole. Sometimes, though, the lies sneak in, and I start to think about my past. I know I am forgiven and redeemed, but that doesn't erase the actions of the person I used to be.

I think about previous dating relationships, and as I reflect, I know that there are some men that do have pieces of me. I feel connected to that individual. Sometimes, it is meaningless because the only thing that was shared between us was a physical moment. The ones that are more difficult to forget are those men who I did let into my heart and not just my body. Those men with whom I formed a soul tie attachment were the men that I connected with on an intimate level that was not necessarily physical.

As you can probably tell, these relationships were not successful; otherwise, this would be a book about marriage and relationships, not rejection and heartbreak. In these soul ties, there were hours of real conversation, moments of genuine caring for each other, and what I believed to be real love. I remember moments when I would think, *This is it. This is what all the romance books talk about. This is my love story, and it is the best one because it is mine.*

Even though time had passed, and I "felt" that I was healed from those relationships, I found out that a part of me was still holding on to them. Some moments were just too precious, and I didn't want to let them be lost or forgotten. The truth is that those moments happened. Those moments are part of me; some of them are milestones in my life. I did not want to forget them. I did, however, grieve them like an actual death. They were beautiful when they were alive and nurturing, but they are gone and not coming back. I thought that if I didn't hold on to those moments or the pain of losing the person attached to the memory, then it would be like if they never occurred.

Now, those relationships ended, and there are no feelings or thoughts of ever going back. I am thankful for the lessons, but still, it is a process of letting go. Lysa TerKeurst says in her book: "It's not supposed to be this way, 'Sometimes, you have to face the death of what you thought your life would be like, in order to receive the blessings that God has for you.'"

Before I fully came to Christ, I had fallen victim to the lies of culture, specifically MTV and rom-coms. I remember idolizing those types of shows and movies, wanting to be like those women who were always partying and having men constantly surrounding them. It always looked so much fun, sleeping around and playing the game.

My heart breaks for the younger me who thought it was okay with giving away her body for such a momentary feeling of gratification of being "loved." That fake replacement love will never even begin to compare just how much we are truly loved by our Father, Creator, and ultimate Healer.

I am still in the process of becoming the woman who God created me to be. I might move at glacial pace, but I am moving. I encourage you to do the same. It all begins with the decision to live a life for Christ. I heard a common saying that I am sure we have all heard, something similar along the lines, "The process is hard, but the answer is simple." It is so simple yet so powerful and applicable to every aspect of our lives.

Crowning Point

Facing the death of my past.

Armor of Choice: Shield of Faith

Knowing to trust that I don't have to know what lies ahead as long as God is the one guiding me.

Verse to Remember

"Brothers and sisters, I do not consider myself yet to have taken hold of it. But one thing I do: Forgetting what is behind and straining toward what is ahead" (Philippians 3:13, NIV).

CHAPTER 17

My Dog Thinks I Am Awesome

I love the way my dog loves me. Without reason, she just does. To her, I am the best part of her day. I don't have to worry about what I am going to wear, how I will style my hair, or if the sushi buffet from Sunday after church is showing on my clothing. None of that matters to her; yet, those are thoughts that are very automatic for most women who I know. For generations, we have been told over and over that we are never enough. We are never pretty enough, skinny enough, Christian enough, smart enough, funny enough, and the list can literally go on forever.

I had been in the process for the last couple of years of transforming myself blonde. I know this may sound vain and insignificant but hear me out. I am a natural brunette. It took me two whole years because I wanted to do it the way that would damage my hair the least. I went through the process of highlights, then retouch of the root, and then more highlights. The process was subtle, but with each time, I was getting closer to my goal: Marilyn blonde. A couple of months ago, my stylist looked me in the eyes and told me, "It's time."

Oh no, I thought. "Are you sure?" I replied. She was referring to the fact that it was time that I bleached my entire hair. After all, the blonde I wanted to be could only be attained by bleaching my hair. It was still a scary process. I didn't know if it was going to look good. Would I lose my hair and go bald? Would I be a Marilyn or a Malfoy?

Guys, I absolutely loved it! The appointment to go that blonde happened to be the same week that my fiancé and I broke up, so naturally, people thought I was having a Britney 2007 moment: the drastic change, not the shaving of my head. I didn't care, though; it was for me. I loved it and was feeling more confident than ever.

Strange things started occurring, though. I totally attribute all these things to "the Marilyn." I noticed that men would do double takes when I walked by. This happened anywhere and everywhere: the gym, the gas station, you name it. At work, men who I had worked with and never once spoken to would come up to me and start random, pointless conversations. They would just talk to me to talk to me. There was power in the blonde; however, it was not good.

Of course, at first, I was excited about the attention I was getting from the opposite sex. It was like an affirmation that I was pretty. I would upload one picture on Instagram, and once it got over ten likes, I was famous. I saw that I wanted that gratification and approval from others. I was finding my worth and acceptance from others instead of the one who made me worthy.

I continued to notice the different ways people would approach me in my everyday life. I slowly began to dread it. I felt ashamed of myself when I saw the lust in men's eyes toward me. I felt naked, even though I would be modestly dressed. My everyday places that used to feel safe were not safe anymore. I received the "attention" that I thought I always wanted at the cost of being constantly objectified. This may not seem like a world-class problem, but it is a hard issue to address, at least for me. The Marilyn look ultimately left me completely baffled and conflicted. On the one hand, I loved the look on me. It was a confidence boost, but I was attracting the wrong type of attention.

Culture historically has a way of telling women how they should think, act, and dress. It is a slippery slope trying to catch up to societal standards placed on women. The beauty industry alone makes around $400 billion a year. There is always a must-have product that will solve all your problems. Today, many people, not just women, suffer from depression and comparison.

Social media is an immensely powerful tool that, if used properly, can be used for the glory of God; instead, we use it to brag and glorify ourselves. We see others' profiles and begin to covet what they have: the house, the spouse, the children, and of course, the labradoodle. We find ourselves envious of that friend who is always traveling the world while you are stuck in your 9 a.m. to 5 p.m. job. It is a constant internal battle because, on one side, you are happy for your friends, but sometimes, doubts and unbelief sneak into our thoughts. The lies that we are never enough are straight from the devil.

I was at a Sunday service, and during worship, God spoke to me. It was not audible. It was more of a vision of me with dark hair and a feeling. Even though I did not hear God's actual voice, this is what I felt was being spoken to me: "My daughter, you are fearfully and wonderfully made. I made you to be you. You are perfect in My eyes. Why are you trying so hard to impress others? I love you. You do not have to convince Me of your worth. I sent My Son to die for you. Is it not My opinion the one that matters? Stop trying to conform to the standards of this world and keep your eyes on Me."

I nearly lost it at worship. I kept thinking about it all day. I was trying so hard to be other people's idea of beautiful when I was already beautiful in God's eyes. I began to think about my future husband, if God did have someone for me. I would want him to be attracted to me for my love of God and not for my hair color. I want him to see me for the me that God created me to be. It is easy to be noticed by the masses for physical attraction, but the man God has for me is going to look past physical beauty and see me for who I really am: a child of God.

The next day, I texted my stylist. "Rachael, I have to tell you something. It may sound crazy, and I know you may be frustrated with me." "What is it?" she replied. I explained, "I feel like God wants me to dye my hair dark. I will explain the details later, but He just revealed it to me. I know we have been working hard to get me this blonde, and you always joked about me never going back to dark, but I feel this is something I have to do." She was fully supportive of my decision, even though she didn't fully understand.

I felt that I had to go through the different hair colors and seasons for God to show me that who I am is all I need to be (this was my personal conviction; because of my heart, dyeing your hair isn't a sin). The more I walk with God, the more I do see His hand over my life. I wonder if He was laughing as I was going through all my different moods and hair colors and if He actually is SMH (shaking my head) at me. God makes all things broken, whole. God makes all things new. God was transforming me, and He still is. I am unfinished until the day of Christ Jesus (Philippians 1:6).

With each time that I draw nearer to my God, He shows me areas that I need to keep improving in. The more I meditate in the Word, the more I can see clearly. I feel that at each stage of my spiritual journey, God gives me what I can handle.

Crowning Point

God is working in me, and He loves me for being me because He made me.

Armor of Choice: Sword of the Spirit (Bible)

I needed to focus on what God said about me instead of what the world made me believe.

Verse to Remember

"Your beauty should not come from elaborate outward adornment, such as elaborate hairstyles and the wearing of gold jewelry or fine clothes. Rather, it should be that of your inner self, the unfading beauty of a gentle and quiet spirit, which is of great worth in God's sight" (1 Peter 3:3–4, NIV).

CHAPTER 18

The Prince and Me Messed Us Up

"Monica, Monica, have a happy Hanukah!" This song from the show *Friends* is on my head after hanging up on the phone with one of my dearest friends, Monica. I was practically squealing out of excitement for her as she told me that her boyfriend was planning a weekend getaway to go stargazing at Big Bend National Park for their anniversary.

We exclaimed, "OMG. OMG! He's going to propose!" Monica and I have been friends since the seventh grade. We were forced into athletics, and we found love and friendship in each other. Even at a young age, we have been the most hopeless romantic women we know. Of course, the harsh reality of men in our life slowly started to chip away at those unrealistic expectations in men; still, we live for Hallmark Christmas movies and rom-coms.

Monica has been in my life through it all. She has witnessed everything from the heartbreaks to all the dress fittings. We basically had our weddings planned on Pinterest before either one of us even had our first kiss. In the time that she has been with her boyfriend and future fiancé, I had gone through the two hardest breakups of my life. She was the smarter one in her choices of men.

Monica, like most of us, had been in a year-long "what are we" type of relationship. The man never defined the relationship because he would claim that he was afraid to get "close" or "attached" because his job had him constantly moving (insert eye roll). Thankfully, my friend knew her worth and decided to end that almost-relationship. It was then that her new and current man came along. I wonder how often in life our blessings miss us because we are still holding on to what we think we want.

When you and your girlfriends are in similar seasons of life, it is the best. You relate to everything; you can plan double dates and weekend trips. You are just so happy that you are both happy, especially when your friend is being treated like the princess that she obviously is. The stars finally aligned in her life, and despite the trials and previous heartaches, her fairytale came true.

My dream fairytale life was within arm's reach. It was right there. I almost had it, but I was yanked from the dream with a spiritual bungee cord wrapped around my waist that had me spinning in every direction. That cord was leading me back to the beginning, to what I thought was ground zero. At first, I was frustrated because I didn't want to go back; I had come so far. I was at my day one all over again. Starting over sucks.

I don't know about you, but I dread the beginnings. I want to fast forward to the results: the relationship, the career, and my happy ending. I could have looked at my circumstances and dwelled in the sadness. I could have chosen to victimize myself and cry out, "Why, God?" But God never says that we won't go through the desert. He never says that we won't go through pain or heartbreak; after all, we live in a fallen world. He does say that He will be with us, though. He commands us to be strong and courageous because He is with us always wherever we go, as shared in Joshua 1:9.

I wouldn't be human if I wasn't heartbroken over losing my fiancé. I could have chosen to wallow and stay sad. I did grieve and accepted the reality. I decided to move forward and rejoice that God was protecting me in the rejection. I couldn't see it then; even now, I don't fully understand, but I don't have to. I had peace about my decision because God goes before us and sees the things we cannot. God does not care about our fairytale endings. He cares about us knowing the truth and living according to that truth.

I want to tell you that God does not waste anything. Even though it may seem that you are back where you started, you are not. When you must start again, you have more wisdom than before and know your areas of weaknesses. You can start in your new beginning and have a new opportunity that is not a setback but a comeback. I was back at the simple pursuit of Him.

God showed me what I couldn't see. Sometimes, it is not as obvious when you are trying to decide which turn to take. One road will not necessarily look spooky, dark, with owls cooing. The other path will not always look like greener pastures, with a flowing river and birds singing hallelujah.

This path I was on was painted to be everything that I had ever wanted. It was all there: the green pastures, the birds, the sunshine, and the husband. It was almost perfect. The more I walked in this life that seemed like a dream, the more I was distracted by the beauty of my surroundings. I was in such awe that I could imagine that is what Alice felt when she found herself in Wonderland. If it wasn't for divine intervention, again, I would have stayed in wonderland, missing the point of my whole life.

When we are distracted by the things of this world, we are susceptible to the temptations of the enemy. Those distractions began to pull me away from my time with God. I felt happy and good to just enjoy being at the place that I was in. I was in love, planning a wedding, and getting married! It was subtle choices of me trading time from spiritual practices for time indulging in the things that had nothing to do with God.

I lost sight of where I was headed and began to drift. Drifting is not noticeable when you are focused on the ride and yourself. It is when you look up and notice how far away you have drifted that we notice the immensity of that "subtle" drift. Often, we drift so far that we can't even see the beginning of where we began to drift. It can be terrifyingly discouraging to think about the work just to get back to where you were to than to continue to work toward the original goal: heaven. As C. S. Lewis once said, "You can't go back and change the beginning, but you can start where you are and change the ending."

I got lost on my drift. The beauty of the drift is that God met me there. He was there to redirect me toward the right way, His way. I was so focused on my fairytale ending that not only did I lose myself, I brought the person on the boat to be cast away with me. I was trying to steer us both in the right direction but ultimately got the both of us lost. I keep thinking what would have happened if we stayed lost. Would we have made our way back to God?

God is and will always be there. He never moved; we did. I subscribe to Hannah Brencher's *Monday Blues* emails. This one email left me speechless. I was convicted. She was talking about how as Christians, we have a savior mentality through which we want to fix and save. In her email, Hannah shared, "Because thinking we can be saviors and lifeboats is so much easier than letting go of someone we learned how to love with our whole body." You are not a lifeboat.

I could take responsibility for my mistakes. I could own my consequences, but why would I bring my future husband down the wrong path with me as well? I had started to depend on him for meeting my needs in every way. When we depend on others to fulfill the needs that only God can satisfy, we are setting ourselves and that person for failure. Our strength comes from the Lord, not our boyfriends or husbands. I had work to do, and so did he. I was trying to change him or, in a sense, "fix" him so that God would bless the relationship and marriage. I read the perfect revelation from Hannah Brencher: "He never became who I wanted him to be. And that expectation I should have never put on him. This expectation that he was supposed to please me with his becoming."

I knew this time I had to focus on my walk alone. I wasn't strong enough to do this walk with him. I would only be able to carry my weight; I had to let him go. As Christians, we are called to love others and to help bring people to Jesus. We cannot do that if we do not take care of ourselves first. We cannot pour from an empty cup.

I also reflected on the following: "We are to love one another, not be one another. I cannot feel your feelings for
you. I cannot think for you. I cannot behave for you. I
cannot work through the disappointments that lim-
its bring you. In short, I cannot grow for you; only you
can."[3]

Letting go is so difficult. It was the most difficult
when I started my walk with Jesus because everything
I was doing before was wrong. I had to learn to die to
myself and my ways in every way. The more I "let go" and
"let God," the easier the whole process became. Surrender doesn't happen overnight. In fairy tales, the ending
is usually the beginning for the princes and princesses.
"And they lived happily ever after." Thanks again, Dis-
ney, for my messed-up perceptions of real love.

Real true love died on the cross for me. Beat that!
Those movies don't show *the after*. Seriously though, I
have some questions: *How do these women keep their hous-
es clean? I am sure those cute little woodland creatures make
more mess than they clean up. Do they have children, and do
their children have allergies from all the animal dander? Do
they wake up five extra hours earlier to exercise, do their makeup, cook, get the kids to school, and then go to work? Are they
like me and wear a messy bun six days a week? When do they
read their Bible?*

---

3 Henry Cloud and John Townsend, *Boundaries: When to Say Yes, How to
Say No to Take Control of Your Life* (Michigan: Zondervan, 1992).

Relationships are messy. It doesn't matter how perfect they may seem; they will require work. There is no perfect fairytale life. There are, however, magical fairytale-like moments in each relationship. This I believe to be true because I have experienced it. I think that God shows us a tiny glimpse of heaven when we fall in love. Not all the relationships are bad, nor will they have unhappy endings; they were simply unhappy because they ended. Some relationships do need to end to lead us to the right relationship.

A relationship with God, like any other relationship, will require work. But friends, the love that we receive on a daily, hourly, or even minute-by-minute basis from God will satisfy you fully, and it will be exceedingly and abundantly enough. I know this is probably the exact opposite of what you want to hear. I know you want a relationship; after all, we were created for relationships. It is okay to have those desires; God gave them to you. I know you want your significant other, and maybe God seems like a consolation price because you may not have that significant other now. Friend, it is the exact opposite. When you experience the love of God for yourself, there is no turning back because God's love is so immense and unfathomable to even begin to describe. I know that if you have felt this, you know. If you haven't, you will. God loves you so much. He is waiting for you. Are you seeking Him to know Him, like stated in Jeremiah 29:13 (NIV)? "You will seek me and will find me when you seek me with all your heart."

Marriage is supposed to reflect the covenant between Christ and the Church. The Church is the bride of Christ. It reflects the love, beauty, and dedication to each other. It cannot be a one-sided relationship. There is beauty when two people share the vision of wanting to live out the purpose that God created them for; that is a marriage worth waiting for.

Crowning Point

It doesn't matter how far you drift; God will always place you back on the right path with so much love and grace.

Armor of God: Helmet of Salvation

If I had renewed my mind and thoughts daily, and I had thought with the truth and had daily mind checks, the drift wouldn't have been so drastic.

Verse to Remember

"You will seek me and will find me when you seek me with all your heart" (Jeremiah 29:13, NIV).

CHAPTER 19

God Does Not Waste *Anything*! (The Dress)

Letting go of the dreams that I had for my future was excruciatingly painful. It was when I realized that if this man was not God's best for me, then the man that God does have for me (if He does) will blow my mind! Who you marry is the second most important decision that you make in your life. Following God is the first.

Knowing this truth did not omit me from the feelings. Our engagement was not on social media, which ended up being both a blessing and a burden. The blessing was that only close family and friends knew. God let me cast all my worries and anxious thoughts on Him as I drew nearer to Him. I was also blessed with the opportunity to heal in a healthy environment without having to give explanations or justifications of why the relationship didn't work. I mourned the relationship with those closest to me. The amount of love and support from my family and friends has been overwhelmingly beautiful, and I can say that I am so well-loved. I am thankful for this season because this was the closest I have felt to God; after all, He heals the brokenhearted and binds up their wounds as stated in Psalm 147:3.

The burden was that because it was not made public, it felt surreal, as if it was a dream that I woke up from in the middle of the night. It did happen, though. I do not want to minimize the relationship or pretend that it didn't happen because it did, and it was beautiful while it lasted. This man and I wholeheartedly believed that we were going to spend the rest of our lives together. Plans were made, venue was booked, and I even picked my dream dress. We could have made the decision to stay together and try to work things out, but it was a very clear-cut, gentle "no."

It was a Wednesday afternoon in December when I was loading my car to go to a "trainer gig." I was sweating because it is Texas, and it is still hot in December. I was simultaneously talking to Jackie; we used whatever pockets of time to catch up.

I needed to tell her about a dream I had about her. I dreamt that I was at a bridal store for a dress fitting, but the dress fitting was not for me. It was for Jackie. She walked out, and her entourage and I were crying because she looked so beautiful in her bridal gown. I was filled with so much joy; one of my best friends was getting married!

"You are going to get married soon," I said as I unloaded the cooler and AED. Her response was, "Girl, thanks, but I am single as a pringle. If it happens, yay, and if not, I am good."

I hung up, and as I was putting my phone away, it rang. I didn't recognize the number, but it was a local area code, so I decided to answer. I heard, "Good evening, Ms. Hernandez. We have great news; your dress has arrived. When will you be available for a fitting?"

My heart sank. I mustered up the courage and agreed to an appointment without saying anything else. I immediately called Jackie back, and she helped me through. I had been dreading this moment, but I knew I had to face it. It then dawned on me. I thought it was funny that I had just dreamt of Jackie in a wedding dress; maybe this was why. My wedding dress had arrived at the bridal shop. Those are always ordered six to eight months before the wedding day because they are made to order. Mine was ready, but there was no wedding planned anymore.

That same Friday, I went to the fitting. I had been in prayer all day, and I asked Jackie and Priscilla to go with me. I didn't know how I would handle or respond to the situation. I was ashamed, embarrassed, and rejected. I kept thinking about how sorry the girl at the appointment would feel for me. I was getting married, and now I wasn't.

I walked into the boutique, and I was suddenly overwhelmed with joy. It was inexplicable, and my heart was so full. The consultant brought me my dress, and I unzipped it. It was just as beautiful as I remembered. I tried it on for closure. I couldn't help but gleam. I wanted to cry but out of joy. My cheeks were hurting from smiling. I healed a little that day. God knew what He was doing, as Genesis 50:20 (ESV) states: "As for you, you meant evil against me, but God meant it for good."

Later, God gave me a dream of me in a wedding dress. It was not the one I had in my possession, and I just understood, "Okay, God, I will give it away."

That same month, the three of us decided to celebrate Christmas in the rain forest, and we went on a girl's trip to Costa Rica. Yes, Costa Rica trip #5. The trip that redeemed all trips.

Before we left, since God had placed it in my heart to give the dress away, I had prayed that it went to someone who really loved the dress and, in a way, deserved it. I wanted it to be a blessing. As women, we know we grow up dreaming of our wedding day and dress, and I wanted it to go to its home. I figured I would contact the designer and do a sort of giveaway. I figured a lot of people loved the dress but maybe couldn't afford it.

Her team was on board, and they were drafting a plan of action.

We were in the chaos of immigration coming back from our Christmas jungle adventure when we all collectively received a text in our group chat. It was one of our dear friends. She was engaged! My first words were, "I can give her the dress!"

A few days later, I called her and bullied her into coming to my house to try on the dress. I had no expectations. I just encouraged her to come try it for her to see if the silhouette was a good fit for her. She arrived. I asked her if she had been shopping. She mentioned that she had started looking online, and she found a style that she loved. "Let me see," I asked. She turned over her phone and showed me a screenshot of the dress she had loved.

My jaw dropped open, and I had a smirk on my face. I unzipped the dress. We both squealed, yes, squealed, with excitement. It was not the same dress, but it was the same type. She was hesitant to try it on, "Andy, I can't. It is so beautiful." I almost slapped her and basically said, "Let me bless you if you love it."

She tried it on, and we both cried. She exclaimed, "This is my dress!" I asked, "Are you sure? If you want to keep shopping, go for it. I don't want to take that experience from you." She replied, "Nope, I am done looking! This is my dress."

I thought, *Wow, God. You are so good! And this dress is going to the best person because she is so loving and caring and giving. You would do it and bless her.*

My friend loves to shop, but she will never pay full price for something. She is very wise in that department, and I thought of the beautiful irony and God's humor. I called the designer's team and canceled the giveaway. They were excited and in shock as well because they said that they had been experiencing delays and reflected that it was so that God would allow me to gift it to my friend.

A few weeks later, she showed up at my house with the dress. She thanked me and said she couldn't keep it. She loved it and wanted it to be her dress, but it was her mom's desire to buy her daughter her wedding dress. I understood: *Okay, God. I tried twice to give it away. I will wait for You.*

That following June, I was at church for morning prayer. I had a vision of a wedding dress hanging. I created a group chat with Jackie, Priscilla, and me. "One of you is going to get married!" I joked with them because of what God had shown me.

We all laughed and started planning each other's weddings. What started out as what we thought was a joke came to fruition real fast. That same day, Jackie had an invitation for "coffee." She was hesitant to believe it was a date because it was her brother-in-Christ, who she had served with faithfully for over six years. They began dating a week later. When they started dating jokingly, I said one time we were having a movie night at my house, "You should try on the dress!" I didn't have to ask her twice. The dress looked beautiful on her, but it didn't close. We just shrugged it off and didn't think anything of it.

That October, Priscilla and I were having an early birthday celebration dinner since she wouldn't be able to celebrate with me on my actual birthday. I was taking a bite of my honey-glazed salmon when both of our phones went off. It was our group chat. It was Jackie, "Guys, I said yes!" followed by a series of pictures of him proposing and her ring. The very next day, she went over to my house to try on the dress. It fit her perfectly. It was her dress all along; we just did not know it.

They decided to get married that December. That was two months from the proposal. God is a God of details, and He works in mysterious ways. He had it all planned out. Bear with me.

Jackie was originally my maid of honor, my best friend, the one who was with me before, beginning, and end of my engagement. She was there to catch every tear, whether happy or sad. When I had gone wedding dress shopping, she knew which dress was the one that was me and which one gave me the most joy. I was conflicted because all the dresses were so beautiful, but I also had the opinions of my bridesmaids, who, of course, I loved so much. I wanted to make everyone happy. She just knew. She cried when she saw me in it; she loved the dress so much. She didn't know she was picking out her wedding dress.

I remembered my prayer: *God, I want to bless someone with this dress, but not just anyone, someone who makes You smile and brings You so much joy. I want the person who this dress goes to, to absolutely love it.* God answered my prayer in the most beautiful way. On December 19, 2020, I watched my best friend walk down the aisle to marry the man who God had for her wearing her dream dress. That dress was never mine. It fit her personality, her character so beautifully: so fun, romantic, and full of love.

God does not waste a hurt. He will turn even our mistakes and disobedience for His glory and for His children, as Romans 8:28 (NIV) states: "All things work together for the good of those who love Him, those who have been called according to His purpose."

Crowning Point

God doesn't waste a hurt. He will turn even our mistakes and disobedience for His glory and for His children.

Armor of God: Gospel of Peace

Walking in the truth and peace of the gospel, sharing God's goodness and faithfulness despite heartbreak.

Verse to Remember

"All things work together for the good of those who love Him, those who have been called according to His purpose" (Romans 8:28, NIV).

CHAPTER 20

Letting God... Really This Time

This series of events happened within a span of one week, and it is something that I am still trying to digest and understand. I feel nauseous now, just thinking about everything that happened. God's love for me is something so immense and unfathomable, and here I am yet again trying to make sense of why He loves me so much. If you are having similar thoughts, let me just save you the trouble. You will not understand this supernatural, never-ending, immeasurable love as much as you try. My advice is to just take it and accept it because you are worth it. Yes, you.

This past Sunday, I woke up dreaming of the man that led me to run to God. It has been almost two years since we broke up. I know what you are thinking because I was too. *Still? Why God? Seriously, like why? What is this man who is practically married all up in my dreams? I do not want him there. I don't even think of him. Again, why? I* felt the sensation of wanting to throw up. I was just fed up and straight-up angry. I was annoyed and frustrated that this specific ex-boyfriend is still a part of my life without being a part of my life.

I bet God was looking at me disapprovingly as I pouted and frowned angrily while brushing my teeth, thinking, *I cannot believe You are doing this to me.* I prayed, as I almost made my gums bleed from brushing too hard: *I am* done! *I do not know what You want from me. I am fed up, God, honestly. Take it! If he was not for me, why is he still there? Take it. Take it! How do You want me to go serve You this morning with this anger and bitterness in me? I trust that You are working for my good, and I know that I do not have to see it or understand it, but I just can't with this anymore.* Take it.

I got dressed and left for church. I usually served with the two-year-olds, then there was a forty-five-minute break until the service where I would go to receive. I would use the break to socialize since I wouldn't see my friends during the week. This time, I didn't feel like talking to anyone, an extremely rare emotion for me. I am not really one to be transparent in my feelings, but people do notice when I am quiet. It defeats the purpose of me trying to be quiet and spend time with God because people come up to me and ask me what is wrong.

In my attempt to avoid people noticing my odd behavior, I made my way into the sanctuary to our usual seats. I opened my Bible and pretended to read it so people wouldn't approach me. I was still in a mood and continued my hissy fit with God. My feelings were hurt, and I wanted to make sure God knew (as if He didn't already).

At the end of the service, our pastor asked us to stand up for prayer. He then asked us to make fists with our hands. He then said, "Whatever it is that you are holding on to, God is saying that it is okay to let it go: that anger, unforgiveness, resentment, that person. It is okay. God is ready to take it if you let Him." He then asked us to open our hands as a physical act of surrendering whatever it was that we were holding on to. I thought to myself one last time and gently whispered, "Take it, Jesus, please." I would like to say that in that moment, I physically felt the release; I didn't.

God is not at our command. He does answer us, but it is in His will and timing. I am so thankful that He did not answer me then and there. He only does perfect works, and Him affirming me then and there would not have been His way of showing me His grandeur. When God shows up, He shows up big!

After our traditional post-church girl's lunch, a few of us headed to a local coffee shop to work on our individual projects (ahem, this one). One of my friends recommended a song to me, so I searched for it on my Spotify account. I liked the song and just kept that same radio playing because each new song that would come out was even better than the previous one. I was still feeling in a weird grumpy mood, so I decided to drive home.

The song "Only One" by Harvest came on during my commute home. The chorus says: "I will remove the names of your lovers, even the memory of their face will fade away, I will write on you my name forever, I will be known by you as faithful and true, so come back, come back, I'll take you to the start, come back come back, I'll take you to your first love."[4]

Tears began to roll down my cheeks at an alarmingly fast rate. I was about to drive through a very curvy road and thought to myself, *This is it. This is how I am going to die, crashing because I cannot see due to the overflowing tears of feeling God's love and mercy for me, worth it.*

I was crying because when I was hearing those lyrics, something happened. The song said, "I will remove the names of your lovers, even the memory of their face will fade away." In that very moment, I tried to think of my exes, and my mind went blank. I really could not remember their names or faces, really! As hard as I tried, I could not remember anything; my memory had been wiped clean. Guys, the love I felt in that moment was indescribable. I did not hear God's voice in an audible way or anything, but I just knew in my heart that it was

4 Harvest, "Only One," track 6 on Curtains, Go Forth Sounds, 2013.

done. They were not there: any ex-boyfriends or "previous lovers." I just knew that in that moment, I was healed. All soul ties were broken. God answered.

Suddenly, like a person trying to find the remote control in the living room, tossing the whole place around, lifting sofas, reaching in those Bermuda triangles in between the cushions, even under the rugs, I tried to search my heart for them, and those men were nowhere to be found. Once my brain fully realized what had just occurred, I let go even more. It got pretty ugly, boogers and all. I prayed: "God, I am so sorry for being angry with You, for doubting You. I know I do not understand most of the time why You do the things You do, and I know that I do not have to. Just *thank You*."

What happened next was not my proudest moment. I know I have plenty of those. God had just blessed me immensely, and after I was able to calm down, the feelings of awe and thankfulness immediately turned to fear. God had just healed my heart, and I went into panic mode. My heart began to feel sadness at the same intensity that I had just experienced His love. God had just delivered me out of what, to me, was an incredible struggle in my life. All the heartbreak and pain in my life can be traced back to the unhealthy relationships with the men in my life, and God just took it like that. How dare He heal me without my consent?

Oh, wait, I caught myself. I had just yelled at God to heal me previously that same morning, but still, I was not ready. Most of my identity was found in these heartbreaks. God took them. I tried desperately to find them. I started to think of memories with those men, and I could not see them or remember them. "Even the memory of their face will fade away." I went from crying in gratitude to crying in desperation, trying to pick up what I had laid down at Jesus' feet.

I wanted Jesus to heal me and take away the memories, and He did. I wanted God to take the hurt and the sadness, and He did. My fear stemmed from the realization that He took the hurts, but He took all the good memories, too. He took beautiful moments that were shared; He took the laughter, the joy, and the love (or what I thought was love). I knew that God had done exactly what I had asked of Him, more even, and I was afraid. I had no problem giving Him the bad memories, but I wanted to keep the good ones for myself. There were some moments that were so sweet, and I remember how special I felt in those moments. I felt that I was loved and that I mattered. I was afraid that if I let them go, I would never experience that kind of love again.

At this point, I was parked crying outside of my house. I did not want to forget how I was loved when I thought I was loved. "God, I don't want to forget," I whispered as both my hands were gripping the steering wheel, and my head was down positioned so that my jeans would absorb the tears. He then spoke to me in the same way He had moments earlier, and the love and peace filled my heart once again.

The tears stopped, and I was okay again. I opened the car door, and as soon as my foot touched the pavement, I knew everything was different, and I was different. I felt foolish for doubting and thinking those thoughts. I was afraid of letting go of these memories with these men because they were instant snapshots of momentary, earthly love. I laughed at myself. I didn't have to hold on to those memories because they remind me of being loved. I am loved. I am worthy. I am a daughter of a King. God loves me so much, and like the great Father that He is, He wants and knows what is best for me. I know that if this isn't His best for me, then I can trust that His best will blow my mind.

God gave me the revelation that it was okay to let these previous relationships go for good. He gave me that blessed assurance that even though there were good memories, they are nothing compared to the love that He offers me each and every single day. He let me know that in order for me to receive the blessings that He has for me, I had to let go, turn the page, cross that bridge, and then burn it without looking back. He was leading me to something better. I do not know what it is exactly, but I let out a sigh of thankfulness and eagerness to step into the next season that God had for me. I was done with this one. Praise God.

God blessed me, but I had to be prepared to change. The rollercoaster of emotions and the drastic changes in my thought process that made me go from a state of thankfulness to fear and worry made me feel ashamed of myself. I spent time in prayer and discernment to try to figure out what prompted those emotions. I came to a sudden revelation that I was the *lame man!* For those of you who are not familiar with this story, let me give you a brief summarization of John 5, "a la Andy."

In Bethesda, there is this magical healing pool. The miracles that come from this pool are basically first-come, first-serve. The first person to take a dip in this blessed pool would be the one to receive the blessings or miracle. I imagine the line to enter the pool like the one of people camping outside of Best Buy for Black Friday.

There was this man who had been "lame" or "paralyzed" for more than thirty-eight years. I have so many questions, but this story is brief, so of course, it leads my mind to wander. This man had been paralyzed for over thirty-eight years, and he had not been able to get in the pool? First of all, how would he make it to the pool every day? Who took him there? If someone helped him get to the pool every day, why wouldn't that person also help him get in line or to the pool first? Even if he did not succeed a couple of times, the man had thirty-eight years to try. Jesus walked by. And, of course, when Jesus walked by, He always had a huge crowd following Him.

When Jesus walked by, the man was begging for money. "When Jesus saw him lying there and learned that he had been in this condition for a long time, he asked him, 'Do you want to get well?' 'Sir,' the invalid replied, 'I have no one to help me into the pool when the water is stirred. While I am trying to get in, someone else goes down ahead of me.'"

When I read this passage for the first time, I laughed at Jesus' question. I thought it would be obvious that this invalid man would want to get better. Who would not want to walk after being paralyzed for that long? It was in a Bible study that one of my friends offered a different perspective of why this man had been paralyzed for that long.

Let us face it. If you or I were in that position, and we were that close to magical healing waters, would we not find a way to get in? I know that when I want something, I rarely stop at nothing to get it. I believe this man was comfortable in his condition. He had the system figured out. He would probably get there early, place his mat down and beg for money from all the people who would travel from great distances to get to this pool. He knew that people were going there for a blessing, and it would make them feel guilty to see a poor invalid man asking for money, therefore prompting people to donate money or goods to him.

When he heard that Jesus was coming, he knew that Jesus would come with many followers. In all honesty, if I were part of Jesus' crowd back then, and an invalid man was asking me for money, even if it was not in my heart to give it, I still would because Jesus was there. I know it sounds terrible, but it's true. In my opinion, this man knew that there would be many people with Jesus and that he would make a killing manipulating them into giving to a poor paralyzed man. He wasn't thinking about Jesus healing him; he only wanted some extra cash in his pockets. When Jesus asked him if he wanted to get better, the man didn't answer. He started victimizing himself and gave excuses that no one would help him into the water. I can imagine that Jesus was somewhat annoyed because He knew what was inside this man's heart when He said, "Get up! Pick up your mat and walk."

I realized that even though I was not in my heartbroken condition for thirty-eight years (thank God), I was like the lame man. Jesus wants us to get better, but He also knows everything that getting better entitles. For the man who had been paralyzed for more than thirty-eight years, he knew that he would no longer be able to rely on his disability as his main source of income. He would have to be like everyone else. He would have to go find a trade or a job somewhere. He would have to earn his income instead of guilt people into giving him money. He would have to try and become a people person. I cannot say for sure, but in my mind, he was rude. I would be rude if I was in that position for that long. People would not even get mad at me for being rude because they would ultimately feel sorry for me. Everything changed for this man after Jesus healed him, but it makes sense why Jesus asked the question if he wanted to be healed. Everything would change for this man afterward.

I had been partially surrendering my past to God. I wanted to hold on to some aspects of my previous relationships because my hurts, in a way, became my identity. These heartbreaks were a part of my past and the reasons why I ran to God in the first place, but I realized that they didn't define me anymore. It's something that happened to me but not who I would always be. God allows us to feel the pain and the hurts, but He does not want us to stay there forever.

God does heal. He healed me. Healing comes at a cost. It means leaving behind your past because that is not who you are, and you are not there. God doesn't remember your past. It is forgiven, erased, and washed clean by the blood of Christ. Nothing can separate you from the love of God, no matter what your story is. God will heal you. He will restore everything that you have lost, maybe not in a physical way, but in an even better way: His way, as Romans 8:38–39 (ESV) states: "For I am sure that neither death nor life, nor angels nor rulers, nor things present nor things to come, nor powers, nor height nor depth, nor anything else in all creation, will be able to separate us from the Love of God in Christ Jesus our Lord."

Romans says that neither present nor future can separate you from the love of God. This means that your past is gone. God does not remember, but we do. I thought to myself, *Why is that?* I think that God allows us to remember so that we can remember Him and His faithfulness. It is up to us whether we use our past for better or whether we stay in the "lame man" mentality. We must take active steps to move forward in the promises and blessings that God has for us. It will be tough, but we have God to strengthen us and lead us to freedom every single time.

CHAPTER 21

MLK Day

Happy Martin Luther King Day. To many, this day is a celebration of a man who peacefully assembled for civil rights and equality. To me, it is the anniversary of the day I was arrested for drinking and driving. This day used to be a day that I wished I could forget for many reasons. I felt so much shame, disappointment, fear, self-hatred. Believe me when I say that there probably isn't a name that anyone can call me that I didn't tell myself.

I had recently turned twenty-one, and I was living in a college town. I was a full-time student, intern, and massage therapy student. I was in a busy season of my life; I didn't have time for anything.

On this particular Sunday afternoon, I was headed home early. I had scheduled my appointments earlier that day, and I was going to home enjoy the rest of the afternoon doing laundry and watching *NCIS*, my guilty pleasure of the time. It was NFL Sunday as well. It was playoffs, and the New England Patriots were playing.

Tom Brady was great then, too. My school friends were shocked that I replied to the calls and messages to join them for the game. I decided to join them because I deserved to do something different than just work and go to school. My gut feeling told me not to go, but I ignored it. I now know that feeling was God's precious Holy Spirit warning me. I should have listened. Thank God that He can turn any experience, circumstance, and season of your life and use it for His good.

I arrived at this local bar & grill to watch the game. I ordered food and an alcoholic beverage, and then another. Everyone was drinking, and as much as I now cringe at my thinking back then, I wanted to fit in. My friends at the time were excited to see me out in the world, and they offered me more drinks. I didn't want to be rude, so I accepted. I should have known better.

Even though my school was known as a "party" school, I had been too busy to do even consider going out. My alcohol tolerance was super low. I had a couple of draft beers and a couple of Patron shots; they were on special, and I felt it as a Mexican duty to show the gringos how to drink a tequila shot like a champ. That night, I lost.

I was having a great time when I received a call from my mom; I stepped outside to take it because I could tell she was crying. She told me that my dad had left again. This time around, I was far away. I couldn't help her; I couldn't be there for her. My heart sank to my feet. I paid my tab and made it to the safety of my massive Ford F150 XL Triton. The tears drenched my jeans in seconds. I needed to go home. These emotions mixed with alcohol became a chemical for disaster. I drove; I couldn't see anything because I was hysterically crying. I lived less than a mile from the bar that I had been at. Unfortunately, proximity didn't matter: I didn't make it home. I didn't see when the light turned red when I hit the car in front of me. My truck received the damage, and I thanked God the person I hit was not hurt. The police arrived, and I couldn't lie. I always thought people exaggerated in movies when they said that handcuffs were too tight; they weren't lying.

I complied with everything that the officers asked and even blew on the breathalyzer, which made for an easy conviction in court. I had a great lawyer, but even with his help, I knew what I had done; I was guilty as sin.

Spending the night in county jail with drunk sorority girls was not even the worst part. The week before that one, I had gotten a small wrist tattoo that read, "Dios Proveerá," which means God will provide. I was doing my best to seek God, but all I knew was go to mass, listen, and leave. I went to mass for an entire year, and not one person ever acknowledged me or said hello; that's what I thought was normal, and that's how I liked it. It didn't bother me because I wouldn't go to church for anyone but for God. I didn't know that for spiritual growth to happen, you need others in your life. The Bible states in Proverbs 27:17 (NIV): "Iron sharpens iron, and one man sharpens another."

There had been no one to grow with to "sharpen" me, so all that I would learn at church, I wouldn't talk about with anyone, much less apply it in my life. I just kept living my life uninspired, unchanged, just focusing on school. While I was in jail, one of the girls that was with me was battling with suicidal thoughts, and I prayed for her. I looked down at my wrist and read my tattoo that was still scarring. The irony of the situation got me laughing: I had been seeking God (well, what was seeking for me at that point in life), and my dad left, and now I was in jail. How was God providing for me? Matters got worse, my program was very strict regarding absences, and the next day was MLK, and there wouldn't be a judge available to release me after posting bail. I thought I was going to be expelled from the program. I complied with fines, lawyer fees, community service, breathalyzer installed in my car (which were very expensive), and I was an extremely broke college student. I didn't want to let my professors know, but I knew it was something that needed to be done immediately. What would I say? "Hi, Dr., I won't be able to make it to clinicals because I need to meet with my probation officer." I understood that these were the consequences of my actions, so I kept moving forward. As much as it was shameful, I took responsibility. I had some time to figure things out because this would come back up whenever graduation came near.

I was in my last semester of undergrad, and to graduate, I had to take my BOC (Board of Certification) exam and my Licensure exam for Texas. My BOC was what I had been studying for the last four years. When it came time to apply, I was denied approval until I met certain requirements. Those requirements were: a letter from an LCDC (licensed chemical dependency counselor) stating that I was in good health and not an alcoholic. A letter from the court, letter from my probation officer stating that I did all that was asked of me, and letters of recommendation to attest to my character. All these requirements triggered an emotional response of that night of the incident. Not only did I not have the finances to be able to meet the requirements (not counting the application fee), I was paying hundreds of dollars for someone to evaluate me because of my DWI. I was labeled as an alcoholic; the system gave me that identity, and that's how the world would see me from now on, even if it was far from who I was. I felt useless and powerless and fell to the floor on my fluffy purple rug broken, wishing God would take me because my life had been a waste and I had no purpose.

The devil would whisper lies of unworthiness constantly during this time, and for a few years, I believed it. I just want to tell you that God will take what the enemy meant for evil and turn it for His good. The mistakes were mine, and there were very real consequences and hardships because of my recklessness, but God kept showing me that with Him by my side, I would be okay. I saw how He protected me in that situation, how He allowed me and the other individual to walk away unharmed.

This situation sobered me both literally and figuratively, and I had to reset my life, reevaluate, and plan for my future. This experience made me strong and resilient, and of course, I made friends all along the way: my probation officer, others like me in waiting rooms, strangers during community service, and even my lawyer became my friend. Because I went through that situation, I was able to relate to others that have also messed up. Our mistakes and failures don't define us. And just like my probation sentence came to an end, I am here to tell you that your probation sentence is at an end, too. There is a light at the end of that tunnel: His name is Jesus.

BTW (by the way): I passed my test, graduated, and am still working in good standing in my profession until this day. Praise God!

CHAPTER 22

Lap Forty (Out of the Wilderness) For Real, For Real...

To quote Britney Spears, "Oops!...I did it again!" Even though I had grown significantly in my walk with God, by my own will, I found myself in yet another abusive relationship. This one almost cost me my life. I ignored *all* the red flags because I fully believed this man was good. He was really seeking God, praying, and doing all the right things "a Christian should do." I knew something wasn't right, but I kept reassuring myself that God was working in his life and that there would be breakthrough.

I kept thinking God could and would do it at any moment. This man had the appearance of holiness that even me, after all the previous lessons, still fell for it. That appearance was only on the outside, though. I liked the fact that people would see him, and they would think that he was a good man. It didn't matter if I felt deep inside that there was something off. I figured none of us was perfect. I mean, I would still struggle with insecurities and old traumas; I can't be the only one.

One night, I found myself curled up in a ball, hugging my knees, hiding from him in the corner of his room. I clutched the Bible I found lying there as hard as I could. I opened it up to Psalm 91 and started praying it over and over again out loud. I was praying it over this demonic presence that was in the room. I was believing God would save me. He was pacing the room back and forth, blocking the door. I couldn't escape. He took my phone. I couldn't call for help. "God, help me," I cried to heaven. I wanted God to open the heavens and physically tell me that He was there and that I would be okay. I wanted an angel to come and fly me out of this place.

Moments before this one, he had thrown me across the room and attacked me. I tried to fight back. So many thoughts flashed through my mind within seconds. *How did I get here? Why did I let get this far? Did I tell my parents I loved them? This is it; I am going home today.* Part of me could not believe this was happening. *There is no way my life became a Lifetime movie.*

I kept waiting on God to save me. I flipped the pages of the Bible. I thought maybe I would look for a more powerful scripture. What I found next broke me, but in a good way. It was a church card. The card I had given him the first time we met. I flipped the card, which said, "Do not be afraid, for I am with you. Don't be discouraged, for I am your God. I will strengthen you and help you. I will hold you up with my victorious right hand."

The moment I read that scripture, I felt God's presence with me. I was no longer afraid. I felt a surge of courage, and I just knew what to do next. God was giving me a way out. He was in shock at what he had done. He was lucid for a moment. I know it was God who was giving me this wisdom and strength because everything in me wanted to do the complete opposite. I listened to him. We slowly made our way to the living room, and I began to encourage him. I told him he needed to eat something, so I ordered some wings for pickup. He was okay with that. I told him that I would go pick up the food, but he didn't let me go alone. He even got off when I went inside to pay.

I couldn't even signal for help to the employees there. I thought, *Okay, what am I going to do now?* He was calm, but it was a matter of seconds before the darkness came back. I drove back to his place but stayed parked in the middle of the street. "You are not going to get off and eat with me?" he asked as he stared out the passenger's seat window. I replied, "No. It is really late. I need to go home. My parents will worry." He began to laugh and said that he knew what I was trying to do, that I was trying to leave him. I reassured him that I was not, and I was just tired and wanted to go home. He said, "Come inside; let's talk." I replied, "No. I am going home."

He slammed his fist against the car door. I jumped and started crying. I thought, *Not again. Jesus, Jesus, Jesus. Give me a way out.* He began to yell and rage in anger as he opened the car door and exited the vehicle. I thought, *This is it, my window of opportunity.* He was stepping out of the car to come around and force me to get off the car, but when he got off, I stepped on the pedal and began to drive off full speed. He managed to jump on top of my windshield and kept telling me to open the door. I told him I wouldn't. The tears kept falling. "Get off!" I yelled back at him.

He locked eyes with me and what I saw still makes me shiver. He smiled. His eyes were pure evil. He began punching my windshield. On the second punch, his fist broke through, and glass was everywhere. I screamed for help, but no one would come. I pressed on the gas drove forward. He fell off the windshield, and I kept driving. I paused when I was far enough to see if he was still lying down on the floor. I saw him get up and then drove home.

I almost crashed because I couldn't see through the tears in my eyes. I kept looking back to see if he was following me, as he was accustomed to. *How was I so dumb to ignore every red flag? Why did I keep forgiving him?*

I parked the car inside the garage, and I could not bear to look at my mom. I didn't want her to know what had just happened. I was okay, physically at least, but more than that, I was so ashamed of what happened to me.

I kept thinking, *It's all my fault. I let this go on far too long. I should have known. My friend was right when she warned me about him, and now, she is not even in my life. He made sure of that. I could have left after the first time he broke my windshield, or the first time he hunted me down, or the time he took my car and drove until I forgave him. How can I even tell anyone? They will only feel bad for me for staying when I should have left. Why did I not just leave? I knew better. Seriously, you were writing about heartbreak and rejection, and you fell for it again, and this time, it almost cost you your life! No one will ever care what you have to say. You just lost all validity because you found yourself in yet another toxic situation. Congratulations, Andrea.*

If you are reading this and find yourself in a similar situation, I want to tell you that you are not alone. God never left you, like He never left me. This was not God's fault. That person who hurt you and showed you what evil is really like was not from God. He was from Satan himself. The devil knows our weaknesses and desires to be loved, so he will send you a wolf dressed in sheep's clothing to destroy you, tear you down, and keep you enslaved.

That is not who you are. You are a child of God. God has a plan. God will heal and redeem you like He is working in me. I was even more ashamed this time because I thought I had overcome this. I thought I was smarter, especially after all those previous lessons. How did I fall for this again? What will people think? Poor little Andy never grew up. She never got it right.

Flashback Moment

God took me back to a memory of when I was little. We grew up in a mobile home community. I have always been an extrovert and have always had a gift for making friends. One afternoon, the neighborhood kids were out playing. My brother, who was older than me but shyer, sent me out to play and meet everyone. He would then go and fulfill his brotherly duties and go "look out for his little sister" but made friends in the process.

Our next-door neighbors had a daughter my age and a son my brother's age, so naturally, it was a perfect fit. She was my BFF, and my brother had a friend. BFF is a loose term, though. You guys know that in order to go into a mobile home, there are steps to get to the actual front door. I believe there are like four steps. I called them stairs.

I would go over to this little girl's house every day to play because my mom never wanted us to have people over. I would have the best day playing with my little

BFF, but every day when I would leave her house, she would push me down the steps! Seriously, every day. I could not understand. I would get mad at her, go home angrily, and swear that I would never ever be friends with her again. My knees and elbows were all scraped. She was evil!

Every night, I would make up my mind to never play with her again, but every morning, she would show up at my house saying sorry and asking if I wanted to play. Of course, I forgave her. I thought I was smarter, though. Now, when I would leave her house, I would tell her, "Please, don't push me down the stairs, okay?" She would nod and agree, but when I would turn around, she would proceed to push me down the stairs. I would be so upset, but the cycle continued.

I decided to be smarter about it. I did not want to stop going over to play, so I had to improvise a plan. When it was my time to leave, I would face her and tell her again, "Please, don't push me down the stairs." She would nod and agree, and I would descend from the stairs facing her straight in the eyes. She would smile and still push me down the stairs! Like how?

I asked my mom if that really happened. God showed me that memory. I didn't think there was a way I was that dumb. My mom confirmed it, though. I was mad at my mother and questioned her parenting skills as to why she let me keep going back every day to play if this little girl was evil. She said she would lose that battle daily with me because I would tell her that I forgave her and that I was extremely stubborn about it. I am stubborn, so this was accurate. I had always been a forgiving person, even as a kid.

I just missed the part where I can forgive but learned not to put myself in dangerous, abusive situations. I always see and believe the good in people. I see them for who they could be and not for who they are. That has been my downfall. I am not Jesus; I cannot rescue or change anyone. Only Jesus can. Pray for me, friends, that I learn this for good. I still struggle.

If you feel sorry for me, it is okay. I do not feel sorry anymore. When I began my healing journey, I started reading many testimonials of women who had experienced similar situations. These women were not just insecure teen girls, as I used to ignorantly assume. They were women from all walks of life, from all socioeconomic statuses and cultures. The devil doesn't discriminate. He wants to destroy all of God's children. "The thief comes only to steal and kill and destroy" (John 10:10, NIV). This next illustration brought so much clarity to my life.

CYCLE OF ABUSE

INCIDENT
Verbal, emotional
and physical abuse.
Anger blaming,
arguing, threats,
intimidation

TENSION BUILDING
tensions increase,
breakdown of
communications, victim
becomes fearful and
feels the need to placate
the abuser

MAKING-UP
Abuser apologizes, gives
excuses, blames the victim,
denies the abuse occurred
or says that it wasn't as
bad as the victim claims.

CALM PHASE
Incident is "forgotten"
no abuse is taking place.
"The honeymoon phase"

1   2   3   4

When I saw the cycle of abuse illustrated, I began to cry. This book is titled *Ugly Cry*, as we have established that there was a lot of crying. I saw the reconciliation phase, and it explained what was going on in my mind and what happened. I was extremely vulnerable and afraid and wanted to believe that he was "genuinely sorry." I thought, *Wow, this is a real thing. I am not alone in this. This is a real problem, so real that there are many charts and articles on it. I was abused, but I am not alone in this. Others have gone through this and have overcome. I can, too.*

And friend, you can, too. Whether you or someone you know is going through a similar situation, there is always a way out. The first step is looking at the signs of abuse and shining a light on these behavior patterns, red flags, or precursors. John 1:5 (NIV) says: "The light shines in the darkness, and the darkness has not overcome it."

God has been working in my life, and He is showing me to draw near to Him. He is enough. He holds me up in His victorious right hand. God wins, period. In imminent danger, His love became my greatest defense. I am His daughter, and even though I fail and I fall, I am falling forward in the arms of my Father. He will be there waiting with His arms outstretched, ready to catch me, each and every time.

This man is walking with God now. God is working in his life, and I know God will have victory over his life. I have forgiven him in my heart, but he is not a part of my life. I tried to hate him, and I did for a while. God showed me that it was not him that I was fighting against. God delivered me from anger at that moment, and His peace came upon me. Ephesians 6:12 (ESV) states: "For we do not wrestle against flesh and blood, but against the rulers, against the authorities, against the cosmic powers over this present darkness, against the spiritual forces of evil in the heavenly places."

Devil, you will not push me down the stairs anymore.

CHAPTER 23

The Real Heartbreak That Began All Heartbreaks

I had been in a discipleship class. My leader, in a beautifully blunt way, said to me, "Andy, I do not know what it is, but there is something that you need to give to God, something from your past, something that you have not healed." My defense mechanism went on, and I wanted to talk back and be like, "You do not know my life!"

I did not know what he meant. I was fine. I was walking in God's will and being obedient, finally! I had even called off an engagement. I knew in my heart that if I got offended, then maybe he was onto something. What did he mean I was not healed? I began to pray a dangerous prayer: "Lord, I do not know what it is. If there is something in my heart that I am trying to hide from You and even from myself, please show me. Speak to me, Lord. Your servant is listening."

I was wide awake at 4 a.m. a few nights later. God woke me up with a heavy "reavy" (revelation) from a dream. In the dream, my dad was leaving us again. This time, it was different; I was a grown-up. He grabbed the keys and was headed toward the door when I said to him, "If you leave again, we won't be here if you ever decide to come back." In my dream, I was so angry, frustrated, and hurt. I said to my dad, "If you walk out that door, this is the last time that you are ever going to see me." I was so angry, and I could feel the feelings in my real self, not just my dream self. I understood that God was showing me that there were a deep-rooted pain and resentment that were still in my heart. I thought that I had forgiven my dad and left that in my past, but God was showing me that I had not fully healed from that.

I was wide awake. In that moment, God took me to a memory of when I was younger. My dad had left us for another woman. I was a tween, and my brother had recently graduated high school and was in a dark season of his life. My mom was too depressed to function, and I had no one. I would ask myself, "How could my dad do that to me? How could my dad leave me?" I loved him more than anything. He was always my teammate; it was me and him against my mom and brother. Even though I did not know why he left my mom, I could un-

FALLING FORWARD

derstand that. I knew many friends who had divorced parents. I knew divorce was common, and I was okay with that if my parents wanted to do that, but why did he leave me? What did I do wrong? Why does my dad not love me? Why did he leave for another daughter?

I was crying at that memory and barely attempting to digest it when God took me back to another memory. I was sitting with my mom one morning eating Reese's Puffs cereal. We were silent. I was still half asleep. My mom was sitting down, staring at her phone. She said out of nowhere, "My phone never rings anymore." I lost it, ran upstairs, and cried my heart out. I knew exactly what my mom meant. She and my dad were best friends. They would talk on the phone throughout the day. He would call her just to see what she was doing, and she would pretend to be annoyed that he always called; yet, every time her phone rang with the ringtone "The Reason" from Hoobastank, her heart jumped. Her phone didn't ring anymore. She didn't have her best friend anymore. That devasted me.

I was crying for her. She was so sad and lonely. I couldn't do or say anything to make it better. *How do you help the people you love when there is not anything you can do?* I cried out to God. I was sad and angry. Then, I remembered and made a personal vow this day. I said to myself: *I do not ever want to feel that. When I am in a relationship, I am going to love so well that I will not get left. I am going to be the best girlfriend and wife anyone could have.* I never wanted to feel someone leaving me as my mom experienced. The very thing I feared happened because I feared it.

The night before this dream, I found myself parked in a truck outside of my house in yet another breakup conversation. I had only begun dating this man, but the red flags were red this time. I was seeing in color. Again, I had found myself in another almost relationship that happened too fast and started off amazing. Like a roller coaster, once we got to the top, everything came down and fast.

Relationships exist for us to sharpen each other, whether they are a friendship or dating. Relationships cause friction and stir up what is really in our hearts. If there are previous hurts and traumas that we have not worked on healing, they will come to the surface. There is a saying that goes, "If you do not make the steps to heal your wounds, you will bleed on people that did not cut you."

We are all humans and make mistakes. Sadly, hurt people hurt people. I was sitting and talking to this man talking about the short-lived relationship and what we learned from it (it was an amicable breakup, and we were able to talk in peace and learn from each other. Not every breakup is healthy, and you do not have to always go and talk to the person). He said to me word for word what my previous relationships have said to me in the past. It was hard to hear, but this time, God was softening my heart to listen and learn. God was showing me that I was not the victim like I had always believed I was. It is always easy to place blame on others when things do not go as planned. It is extremely difficult to look at ourselves in the mirror and realize that sometimes, we are our own worst enemy.

The conversation continued. He said that I was "perfect," he didn't think he could do better, and that I was the best. He said that he realized that because of this relationship, he knew that there were parts of his past that he had not let go of and forgiven. We both agreed that we got carried away and rushed into a relationship with the best expectations, but ultimately, we realized that neither of us was ready to be in a relationship with another person until our hurts were healed and our relationship with God was first above everything else.

Rejection stings. The lies of the enemy are the first to pop into my head. He says things like, "You obviously are not perfect. You are not enough. He is lying to you. You are not worthy of being loved. No one cares about you. Everyone will always leave you." I would think to myself that if I was sooooo perfect, why was I so easy to leave? I always gave my best in relationships, I gave my all, and still, I was left all alone.

If you have not read Gary Chapman's *The 5 Love Languages*, I highly recommend you do. He talks about the five love languages, which are basically how we humans show love and are loved by others. They are words of affirmation, touch, acts of service, gift-giving, and quality time. These are our love languages but based on our values and upbringings. There are a couple that may be more dominant over the others. For me, I feel loved when someone gives me quality time and words of affirmation. I see time as a precious gift, and if you are giving me yours, that means the world to me. I learned that words were powerful in my life as well. Words of worth and encouragement were never spoken to me at a young age, so when someone speaks life into me, my soul feels nourished. Those are the two dominant ways that I feel loved and affirmed, even though they are all important.

I realized, though, that when I am in a relationship, I love hard. I love with all the love languages because I know what it feels like not to feel loved or affirmed, so I want to make my partner know that they are loved. I don't want them to have one doubt about where I stand on my feelings and convictions for them. I started to analyze why I was like this. Was it possible that I loved too hard that I pushed this person away? Yes, absolutely. Again, the very thing that I feared came true because I feared it. I had a heart tug, and I understood. When I love, I overlove. I am not saying that loving too much is a bad thing, but for me, it was the intent behind it. I had a heart check.

My fear is people leaving and taking their love with them. In my mind, I thought if I did everything right and loved hard, there was no way anyone would ever leave me. Plot twist: everyone left, and they left freakishly in the same way. These men in these relationships, regardless of duration, were so well-loved by me. I was loving that hard because that was the love I wanted and expected in return, like a transaction. I would find myself so crushed and disappointed that not one person from my past cared enough for me to love me according to my love languages. I realized I placed impossible standards on these men who were broken, like me. I was longing for that sacrificial love and affirmation that I was loved and worthy. I was looking in all the wrong places.

In my profession, I constantly see running T-shirts with the quote, "F.E.A.R.," which has different meanings. One meaning I have seen says "forget everything and run." Another meaning reads "face everything and rise." The answer had been in front of me all along, and I kept missing it. After every broken relationship, there has been a lesson: Matthew 6:33. Instead of running to God, I would forget what I learned and run toward someone else. How long am I going to keep running from God and the relationship that is the ultimate love? He has been a part of my life, and by His grace, I am here today, but when is *He* going to be enough? I have kept running toward relationships with men who will disappoint me, hurt me, and leave me. Instead, I should be running to the one that will never leave me, as Hebrews 13:5 (NIV): "Never will I leave you, never will I forsake you."

The one who loves me calls me worthy, fearfully, and wonderfully made. Guys, if words of affirmation are your love language, please open your Bible and read what God says about you. The entire Bible is a love story for you! Why do we let men or women dictate our worth and identity instead of believing who God says we are?

I was talking to my friend, Priscilla, as tears were falling from my cheeks. "Dude, I feel like I keep going through this cycle of rejection until I finally learned my lesson that God is enough. I know it took me years, but I get it. God was and still is so patient with me."

I once heard a preaching on how life is a test. God is the teacher who is silent during the test. This teacher, however, does not give us grades; instead, He gives us grace and infinite retest opportunities. To Him, it is not a failure. He wants us to really learn the lesson, and unfortunately, how fast we learn the lesson is entirely up to us. It took the Israelites forty years to enter the promised land when it was a journey that should have been less than two weeks!

I know I make mistakes, but I pray that it does not take me forty years to listen and be obedient to God.

Still, He waits, corrects, and loves. Finding myself in this cycle of rejection, I understood that everything I wanted and expected from these relationships was what God wanted from me. I was so devoted, faithful, and loving in these relationships, while the relationship that mattered the most was always on the back burner.

I felt that God was telling me, "That rejection you feel from them is what I feel from you." When He said this to me (not audibly), I was broken. I had to be honest with myself and ask, "Do I really love Jesus, or do I love how He loves me and all He does for me?" I was ashamed to even think it because I did not want to admit to myself that I was more selfish than I thought. Then, I realized even if I do not think so, God knows my heart, whether it is selfish or not, and He doesn't care. There isn't anything that I can do for Him to love me any less. I asked God why I could not love Him the way that He loved me. "Because you didn't choose Me; I chose you."

The more I fall in love with Jesus, the less I feel the pains and rejections of the world. The more I fall in love with Jesus, the more I trust in His plan and will for my life. Was I sad that my relationship had ended? Of course! I was at peace this time because I knew that there would not be a worldly relationship that would satisfy me until I am fully satisfied with my relationship with God.

Rejection stings. Yes. However, we will never be rejected like Christ was. He knows the pain and sorrow better than we could ever imagine. He chose to carry His cross rejected to die for you and me. As I continue to walk with Christ, He simultaneously continues to work in me. I went from being cheated on, to not being worthy enough, to breaking off an engagement, to being humiliated in front of my parents, to being too "perfect."

Although these rejections had the power to destroy me, God was using them for His glory. If rejection were a muscle in the body, I would have exercised it many times and have built endurance. I do not think that I have fully grasped it, but I understand it better. I know that rejection is also God's protection. We are stubborn humans, and without divine interventions at times, we will willingly stay in relationships that will lead to death. Instead of being the victim and believing the lies of the enemy, I took those thoughts captive and made them obedient to the name of Jesus Christ. I began believing that I was who God said I was. God was not punishing me; He was pruning me. Like a father disciplines a child, God disciplines us for our own good. We may not like it, but we must trust that it is for our own good because we cannot see what God sees, as Hebrews 12:6 (ESV) states: "For the Lord disciplines those whom He loves."

God is omnipotent and goes before us. He knows that there are some roads that we will take that are wrong for our purpose. Hebrews 12:11 (NIV) says: "No discipline seems pleasant at the time, but painful. Later on, however, it produces a harvest of righteousness and peace for those who have been trained by it."

I felt that at this point in my life, I finally understood the training. God said I was His child, a new creation, without blemish, white as snow, worthy, and loved. I didn't need to go searching everywhere else to find that. All I needed to do was come to Him. He did not care that I was a mess, that I fail Him daily, and that I will fail Him again. I will never be able to love God as much as He loves me because there is no way, but I want to try to love Him even more. The Word says, "If you love me, you will obey my commands."

God is a perfect gentleman, so kind and patient, waiting for His bride. My friend Caleb explained this once so brilliantly that I knew it was a revelation from the Holy Spirit. He was leading our discipleship class. His smile was radiating joy when he shared. This was his revelation: "Marriage never made sense to me. I come from a divorced household. I didn't quite get what it meant when Jesus was referred to the bridegroom. But now I get it. You see, the cross is Jesus' proposal to me. When I accepted Christ into my heart, and I was fully sold out on Him, that is when He put a ring on my finger. I am His. We are engaged, I am His bride, and He is my bridegroom. I am engaged to Him. I am going to live in a way that is going to honor Him until He comes back to marry me."

When He said this, my jaw dropped. I could not help but smile because it made sense. I understood. At this moment, I felt a peace upon me. I was always shamefully worried that God did not have a husband in His will for my life. I would think, *Okay, God. Yes, You are enough for me, but I still desire a husband.*

That afternoon, I could not stop smiling because I knew that even if God did not bring me an earthly husband, I already have a bridegroom waiting for me to be His wife. I am engaged to Jesus! I know that is crazy to say. I would have rolled my eyes at myself five years ago, but now, I cannot help but gleam at this beautiful revelation. God is enough.

As for my dad and me, God restored our relationship. He allowed us to have a tough yet healing conversation. I told him how much his leaving affected and hurt me. I told him how it led me to attempt to fill that void with relationships that still left me feeling empty. I told him that he was the first man to break my heart. He was quiet, listened, understood, and cried with me. Our Heavenly Father is loving on both of us and restoring us as individuals and as a family. That kind of love can only come from God Himself. We must forgive the unforgivable because God forgives the unforgivable in us every single day.

Friends, there is nothing from my story that makes me special or makes my story better than yours. What makes all our stories beautiful is God's unfailing love and redemptive power toward His children. If God can work in my life, He can work in yours. There is nothing you have done that God cannot forgive or redeem. He wants you. He is calling you. God longs to show you His grace, mercy, and unfailing love. This is just the beginning.

Tag! You're it.

About the Author

Andrea was originally born in Reynosa, Mexico, but was raised in the Rio Grande Valley in the wonderful city of Mission, Texas. She is a graduate of Texas State University, where she received a bachelor's degree of science in athletic training. Andrea also attended the Lauterstein-Conway Massage School and Clinic in Austin, Texas, to become a licensed massage therapist. After her schooling, she moved back to the Rio Grande Valley to work as an athletic trainer at the high school level. It was during this time that she encountered God in a supernatural way that changed her life. She began to walk with the Lord, which then allowed her to grow in her gifts and talents and be able to serve God and her local community. She is currently attending seminary school at Rio Grande Bible Institute and volunteers in different ministries at her home church, New Life Family Church, in McAllen, Texas. Andrea's hope is that others will be encouraged to draw near to God throughout her testimony so that they, too, can experience freedom, blessings, and the ultimate love of God.